Morning Breeze

———————

拂 朗

Morning Breeze

A TRUE STORY OF CHINA'S

CULTURAL REVOLUTION

by Fulang Lo

CHINA
BOOKS
& Periodicals, Inc.
San Francisco

Cover Photo by Carol Moilon

Cover Design by Robbin Henderson and Dina Redman

Illustrations by Jie Dong Lo

Library of Congress Catalog Card Number: 89-60225
ISBN 0-8351-2125-9 (cloth)
ISBN 0-8351-2126-7 (paper)

Printed in the United States of America by **CHINA BOOKS** & Periodicals, Inc.

Acknowledgements

This book is dedicated to Dr. Myra Sklarew, the former director of the MFA program of the Department of Literature at The American University in Washington, D.C., and to Mr. Budd Getschal. Their belief in me, their consistent encouragement and generous help made this book possible.

I want to thank all the administrative staff at The American University; the Center for International Students, and the Department of Literature. I particularly thank Mr. Joe Neal and Ms. Colette Nozicka, the former and current directors, respectively, of the Center for International Students; Mr. Wade Davenport, my former academic adviser; Dr. Edward Kessler, the Chairman of the Department of Literature; Professor Henry Taylor, the Director of the MFA program in the Department of Literature; Professors Robert Bausch, Kermit Moyer and Stephen C. Grede.

Many thanks must also be given to Dr. Philip Singer and Dean Joel Russell of Oakland University for their great help in bringing me to the United States.

I owe a permanent debt to Professor James Schlesselman, of the Uniformed Services University, and his family, for accepting me as an honored guest and teaching me to use the computer.

For their friendship I thank Mr. Philip Moore and his family, Mrs. Katherine Donavan, Ms. Laurie Burch, Dr. Samuel Dove, Mrs. Samuel Dove and Mr. Thomas V. Alexander.

I am grateful to China Books, Mr. Foster Stockwell, and most especially, Ms. Nancy Ippolito.

Finally, I wish to thank my editors, Carol Eron and Bob Schildgen, for their sensitive and beautiful understanding of this book.

Contents

Libraries were going to burn books.

CHAPTER 1

Layers of Heaven

人重天

Stretching along the banks of a river, my native city is surrounded by green mountains covered with sugar cane and corn plants. Neijiang, a medium-sized city, lies between Chengdu and Chongqing in the southwest province of Sichuan. The river that winds through the city and the valley is a branch of the Yangtze, called the Snake. It shimmers with white clouds and blue sky. Large ferry boats on the river sometimes join together forming a bridge, and I often walked across this bridge to my school. Here is where I spent my happiest years, with my two best friends Meimei and Suansuan.

I met Meimei on my first day at the Neijiang Dragon Gate High School, where she was standing on the playground holding two ping-pong paddles. "Play ping-pong?" she asked. Before I could say yes, she handed me a paddle, and we played all morning and became friends. I asked,

"How old are you?"

"Fourteen," she said. "How old are you?"

"Fourteen, too."

Meimei was a very good ping-pong player. Her paddles never left her hands, and wherever she went she bounced on her toes ready to play.

Meimei was tall and thin. She always wore a purple T-shirt, white pants, and white sneakers. Her hair was cut short above her ears, and her skin was honey-colored. Her eyes were round and dark, with long curved eyelashes. Meimei was beautiful.

Meimei had a flute, which she played on her way to school in the morning and on the way home. Sometimes I met her, and asked, "What is the song you are playing?" She always answered, "Birds singing."

Suansuan, my other friend, was aloof. Her habit was to sit alone in a corner of the classroom and write poems. She wore thick glasses, and was the only student in our class to wear them. Suansuan was short and a bit chubby. She never cared about her dresses, and many times she wore her socks inside out. She didn't take me as her friend until the first exam scores were posted and I scored highest in English. She spoke to me quickly in a flat voice: "Will you go with me to the Small Town Inn to have rice wine and cold beans? We can take a boat."

The green mountains seemed to move as the boat glided between them. At the foot of the mountains straw cottages were scattered, large and small. Around the cottages bamboo trees rose up like walls.

The inn, a large sky-blue pavilion, was old and as quiet as a Buddhist temple. The only waiter, an old man with a long white beard, served us bowls of wine and seven small dishes of cold beans. Suansuan said, "Two plus seven is nine. The number nine symbolizes good luck. In ancient times people believed the sky was formed by nine layers and over the ninth layer was Heaven."

Suansuan pointed out the window at the mountain and said, "That mountain by the Snake River is called the Tortoise. Because the tortoise and the snake are symbols of longevity, the inn was named 'Longevity.'"

The rice wine was sweet, more like a dessert than wine, and fragrant too, like jasmine. Counting the beans in the dishes, I found that each had exactly twenty-seven beans. "Twenty-seven is three times the number nine. This means good luck, too," I thought and smiled. No wonder the boatman had charged us exactly nine cents to get here.

"I come here to write my poems," Suansuan said and stood up. Lifting her small bowl, she made a toast:

> Drink up, life is wine.
> Do not wait, it's time.
> Drink, drink, life is fine!

Meimei lived near the school in a large brick house. She liked the Small Town Inn too. She often flew kites around Tortoise Mountain and went fishing in the Snake River. I spent a summer vacation at her home. She and her mother lived alone. I didn't see her father, who worked far away in the south of China.

Meimei's mother was kind. She cooked for us and washed our laundry. She enjoyed watching us play ping-pong in the yard, and when she found time she made us big dragon kites. I loved her, and always wished she were my mother.

Meimei played ping-pong two-handed. She taught me how to use my left hand also. "First, learn to swing your left arm," she directed. "Second, handle chopsticks left-handed at meals." Gradually, my left hand became skillful, and we played double games with four paddles. That was great fun!

We fished in the cool early morning. Sitting by the river, we waited patiently and caught fish. Meimei said, "To fish is an excellent way to teach yourself to be patient. Patience is important for everyone." Sometimes we went quite far and fished in a mountain pond. Meimei told me she had once caught a little yellow fish there with four legs. "But I returned it to the pond," she said, "A strange fish is usually poisonous."

Suansuan liked to invite me for dinner at her home, an apartment with four rooms, very much like mine. Her parents were professors at the University of Agriculture. At their dinners the table was set in a festive way with white silk napkins, silver spoons, and ivory chopsticks. We were not allowed to talk while we ate. Instead, we listened to light music. After dinner we all went out for an evening stroll. Her parents were familiar with all our school books and asked me what subject I liked the best. They told me I was welcome to read in their library, which contained many novels.

Suansuan's parents called her "Erzi," which means "Son." They called Suansuan's younger sisters, "Number Two Son" and "Number Three Son." They must have wanted sons, I thought.

My mother did not like me to invite my classmates home unless they were poor. "Don't show flowers to the rich, but send charcoal to the poor," she always said. She was my stepmother. My own mother died when I was four. My father met my second mother at his office when he worked as a statistician and she, as an accountant. Later, my father got a new job as a supervisor for the largest industrial equipment manufacturer in our region. Then, my mother got a job in a shipping company on the same street. They both got higher wages. My father was a good humored man and he loved her very much. She loved him too. They never quarrelled. They didn't pay much attention to me, but they never spanked me either; I was their "good child."

Our teachers were fond of Meimei. She was a wonderful athlete and good at mathematics. In everything, she was quick and precise. They also had a very high opinion of Suansuan, our class scholar. They said, "Suansuan is the most talented student we have ever had since the school was established in 1955. She is at the top in all subjects. Her literary writing is the best." My teachers liked me because I was good at language, art, and history. And I had the ability to organize the students. Shortly after I entered the high school, I became a leader in the Student Union. Our teachers said they were sure that we three would be accepted into the finest universities in China, Qinghua or Beijing University.

Three years passed quickly. Both Meimei and I were seventeen and Suansuan was eighteen. Meimei wanted to become an engineer, Suansuan, a writer, and I, an artist.

On May 16, 1966, I arrived at school and found all the students and teachers gathered in groups here and there on the campus, writing big signs. They wrote, "LONG LIVE THE PROLETARIAN CULTURAL REVOLU-TION!"

"What's going on?" I asked the class monitor.

"The Cultural Revolution has begun, and it's going to destroy the old educational system."

"Why is that?"

"The old methods have been producing bourgeois intel-lectuals. Read today's newspaper! Today the great Cultural

Revolution begins!"

I picked up the newspaper from the ground and saw the first page splashed with headlines. One said: "COMRADES, JOIN THE GREAT CULTURAL REVOLUTION LAUNCHED BY OUR GREATEST LEADER CHAIRMAN MAO HIMSELF!"

As I was wondering why the headlines emphasized the words "Chairman Mao himself," the school emergency bell rang and we all proceeded to the playground, where the teachers stood on the stage. Their expressions were particularly serious. The school principal began the meeting by announcing:

> The great Proletarian Cultural Revolution is an unprecedented revolution in Chinese history, launched by our great leader Chairman Mao himself. This revolution has far-reaching significance, which will be corroborated by Chinese history. From now on, teachers will stop teaching and students will stop studying. All must devote themselves to the revolution. The National Examination for College Entrance scheduled for early July has been postponed.

The Communist Party Secretary of the school walked to the microphone and announced in a loud voice, "The Great Proletarian Cultural Revolution is a test for everyone. It will distinguish stone from gold and separate the fish eyes from the pearls."

I felt disappointed that the examination was postponed. I looked over at Meimei. She lowered her head. I looked at Suansuan. She gave me a spunky smile, as if nothing had happened.

After the meeting we were told to go to our classrooms to make big signs expressing our attitude towards the Cultural Revolution. We found all the benches in the room piled up, and the tables joined together, creating one big table. Our master teacher came in. He carried a thick roll of white paper, ink bottles, and writing brushes. In a meek voice he said, "Write, I will get you more paper."

Before noon, our classroom was covered with posters. I looked at the newspaper headlines and copied one in ancient Chinese calligraphy. I signed my name and went home for lunch.

The next day most of the teachers seemed to have disappeared. A rumor spread that they had gone to Number 2 High School to study new policies. For the next twenty days we came to school and had nothing to do but make big posters and read the newspapers. One day the newspapers printed this from Chairman Mao: "All Chinese must criticize the old play, *Magistrate Hairui Loses His Position.*" None of us had seen the play, so we didn't know what to say about it. Suansuan, however, had read it, and she whispered to me, "Hairui was a well-known magistrate in the Ming Dynasty four hundred years ago. According to the play, he loved the people and tried again and again to persuade the emperor to be merciful, and for this reason Hairui was considered a troublemaker, a disobedient magistrate. He lost his position." We didn't understand the reason for Chairman Mao's directive, but we had always been taught to follow any directive by our government leaders and had never questioned this. So we all designed big posters with quotations from the newspapers attacking the play.

Meimei became silent. She didn't play ping-pong anymore. Instead of her purple T-shirt, she wore a black blouse. One afternoon I suggested we go fishing together, but she said sadly, "I'm afraid I can't be your friend anymore because I am from a capitalist family. It would get you in trouble." Before I could stop her, she ran off.

I didn't believe Meimei was from a capitalist family. A capitalist child would be spoiled. Meimei was not spoiled. A capitalist home would have many servants. Meimei's home had none. Meimei's mother had washed my clothes and cooked for me when I stayed with them. I couldn't believe her mother was a capitalist. She was a good woman, a kind woman. She was the best mother in the world!

I went to see Meimei later that day. She was not home. Her mother explained to me why they were labeled a capitalist family. "When Meimei's father was a child he worked in a tobacco factory. He worked for his boss for nineteen years. The boss was an old man who had no children. Before the old man died, he adopted Meimei's father. He left a will that said, 'I give my house and factory to this young man. In return he must take care of his adoptive mother and support her until she dies.' Because of the house and the factory, my family has been listed as a capitalist family. But we don't own the factory. It was taken over by the government many years ago."

At a school meeting on another day, a student from a poor peasant's family made the following speech:

> The first goal of the revolution is to clarify class lines. Those who are from the poorest peasant families or the poor factory workers' families are the Red Sort. They are revolutionaries. Those who come from a capitalist family or a landlord family or a well-off peasant family are the Black Sort. They are enemies. The rest are the Gray Sort, who will either be revolutionaries or enemies—depending on their attitude towards the revolution. If they stand on the side of

the revolution, they will become revolutionaries. Otherwise they will be enemies. From now on, the Black Sort are not allowed to smile or to cry. Their smiles mean they are laughing at the revolution; their tears are shed for their lost past. The Black Sort are not allowed to sing songs because their voices are poison arrows directed towards the revolution.

Suansuan and I both were considered the Gray Sort, although my family background was regarded as less dangerous than hers. My parents were not professors—who were called Reactionary Academic Authorities—and they had no religious beliefs. All religious groups were labelled "Reactionary Guilds." Suansuan's grandfather was religious; he believed in Buddha.

Suansuan ignored the Cultural Revolution as much as possible. It didn't matter to her who the Red Sort or the Black Sort were. She still went often to the Small Town Inn and wrote poems.

One evening Suansuan came to my house to tell me that the libraries of the University of Agriculture were going to burn books. Literature books, art books, and music books—all were called "Poisonous Grasses" and were being thrown out of the library! She said the pile of books was as high as a mountain.

"Why don't we go take them when no one is watching?" she said. It seemed like a good idea, and, when I agreed, she smiled and quoted an old saying: "A scholar who steals books should not be called a thief."

That evening we went to see the mountain of books. There was no guard there, so each of us filled a schoolbag with books. On the road near our homes, we laid out all the books in the moonlight and divided them evenly. One of the best books I got was *Art Philosophy*. It was filled with nearly a hundred pictures of oil paintings neither of us had ever seen before. Suansuan found a most wonderful novel, *Marx's Youth*. It described the romantic love between Marx and his fiancee. We could hardly believe the great founder of Communism had had such a private life.

There were only four students in our class qualified as the Red Sort. They established a revolutionary organization called the Red Guard, just as students in the cities of Beijing and Shanghai had done earlier. The government newspaper reported, "The Red Guard Organization is new and vital. The Red Guards are iron fists. The Red Guards are Generals of Heaven. The Red Guards will defend our great leader, Chairman Mao. The Red Guards will sweep dirty old water from the earth. The Red Guards will destroy the old world and create a new world."

The four Red Guards at our school wore red arm bands, and painted new slogans everywhere on the campus:

"THE DRAGON'S SON IS A DRAGON, A PHOENIX'S SON IS A PHOENIX, BUT A RAT'S SON CAN ONLY DESTROY THE GROUND BY MAKING HOLES IN IT!"

"MY FATHER IS A HERO, SO I AM A HERO; YOUR FATHER IS A BAD EGG, SO YOU ARE A BAD EGG!"

"BLACK SORTS, RAISE YOUR HANDS! IF YOU DON'T OBEY, I WILL SLAUGHTER YOU!"

The Red Guards in my class had actually been dull students who got the worst marks. I felt they welcomed the Cultural Revolution because it abolished the university entrance examination, which they probably could not have passed. The Red Guards began holding political meetings at the school, and everyone was required to attend. Their first lecture was called "Revolutionary Family History Education." They preached to us about their own bitter family backgrounds.

A female Red Guard appeared first on stage. She said, "My father was a rickshaw-puller. One summer noon, he pulled a rich couple uphill. It was hot, and the sun was like fire. He was tired. He strained to pull the rickshaw. Suddenly his bladder dropped out. The urine wet his pants."

When she sat down the other guards cheered.

A male Red Guard then spoke, "My father lived in a shabby straw hut. One night it caught fire. My father fought against it. He fought all night. The next morning his tooth ached. He had lost the ability to bite a pickled cucumber."

Suansuan burst out laughing. I knew she was laughing at the two stupid speakers and their fathers. I bit my lip to control myself, or I would have laughed out loud too. Meimei lowered her head. She was not allowed to express emotion. All the Black Sort lowered their heads like Meimei. There were seven. Most of my class were Gray Sorts—there were forty-five of us.

The school Communist Youth League secretary was a Gray Sort, too. Her father was a wine-seller and her mother a butcher. She followed the Red Guards around, flattered them and parroted their words. One day she created a huge poster. It read, "I would rather have my head cut off than not defend the great Mao Zedong's thought!" To show her determination, she bit her index finger and smeared blood on the poster. Overnight, her action earned her the title "Woman Hero," and made her a favorite of the Red Guards. To memorialize the occasion Suansuan wrote a poem dedicated to her:

> Daughter of a wine seller,
> Daughter of a butcher,
> A grin on your face,
> A knife in your hands.

11

Meimei kept her head lowered all day long. She refused to talk to me. One afternoon I found her alone in the school bathroom. She tried to run out. I grabbed her. I saw that her eyes were red and tearful. Again she ran off, and I could not stop her.

Walking home alone, I stopped at the river and took a boat to the Small Town Inn. I sat by the window, thinking of Suansuan's poem for Meimei:

> Lift your head high like a stallion
> Young one.
> Do not bow down under your burden.

"Burden?" I said. "It's not a burden. It's a mountain. Meimei carries a mountain which I can see but cannot help remove." Out the window the sunset was dim and red and made the river look like blood.

In July, the school principal announced a new order from the local government, "Two-thirds of the high school graduates are to go to isolated mountain villages to lead the Socialist Education Movement, to 'spread revolutionary seeds.' One-third of the students are needed to stay at the school."

Suansuan and I were listed in the group that was leaving. But Meimei was not going. All the Black Sorts like Meimei were put in small groups, which had four Red Guards, Black Sorts, and eight Gray Sorts. The Gray Sorts in Meimei's group were of a special type, like the Woman Hero, whose name headed the list.

The night before we left for the mountain villages, Suansuan and I decided to say goodbye to Meimei. We wanted to promise that we would be her true friends. We wanted to give her half of the university books we had saved from the burning. We wrapped them in newspapers that were

12

filled with revolutionary headlines so that they wouldn't cause her trouble.

Her house was dark; nobody was there. We waited for nearly two hours. Finally we knocked on the neighbor's door. The neighbor told us that Meimei and her mother had moved away and had left no address. The commune officials had ordered them to leave, and the house was going to become the commune office the next day.

We left early in the morning. It was raining. A muddy truck took Suansuan and me and another thirty-six students away. Suansuan sat beside me. We didn't talk. The truck passed by the Small Town Inn, the Snake River, and Meimei's house, which grew smaller and smaller and then faded away.

"Breeze, Morning Breeze, you are beautiful. . ."

CHAPTER 2

Wash Hands and Wash Feet

洗手洗脚

It was two o'clock in the afternoon when the truck stopped in Ganyang city, 100 miles to the west. We had been in the truck for six hours. A short, middle-aged man received us, an intellectual. "I am the Mayor's secretary. Welcome. You will stay here for nine days of training, then proceed to mountain villages to spread revolutionary seeds. This is the way for you to carry out the Socialist Education Movement." He spoke with a smile and pointed out two classrooms for us to stay in, one for the boys and one for the girls. He distributed food coupons to us, and instructed us to be in the auditorium at eight next morning.

As we opened our bedrolls and spread them on the floor, we saw other groups of students arriving and heard the secretary repeating his welcome. The students were from other cities far away.

It was too early for supper, so after a shower, Suansuan

and I decided to go for a walk. The town was small. It had only one street. At the end of the street, stood a white tower, narrow and very high. Beside the tower we noticed a sign that read "White Tower Temple." Under these characters was a line of smaller characters: "The White Tower Temple has controlled the River Spirit for a thousand years." We both laughed. The river behind the tower was wide and strong, a branch of the mighty Yangtze. How could the little tower control it? Suddenly I felt sad. The river reminded me of Snake River, of Meimei.

The next morning, in the auditorium, the Mayor's secretary announced who the student leaders would be. Each school had one, and I was declared the student leader for our school. After that, he asked us to go to an adjacent room for a meeting.

Two men sat in there, young and energetic-looking. They wore starched military uniforms. They stood up when we entered, shook hands with us, and told us they were Deng He, and Yong Tian, students of the Radar Military Academy in Chongqing. And they had been assigned to the He Feng commune to carry out the revolution fifty miles away.

"We have been assigned to train you," Deng He said, "and teach you the four military principles: be united, alert, serious, and strong. We ask you, the student leaders, to wake up your students every morning at six so they can do exercises. There will be ten minutes for breakfast, and then bring them to the auditorium at eight. We'll teach you how to lead the revolution in the countryside. The class struggle is complex, and so you must be very careful." Before the meeting was dismissed, Deng He opened his notebook and read off our names. As he called mine, he looked up at me.

We walked back to the auditorium. Just before I entered,

Deng He stopped me and asked, "Could you tell me, what is the meaning of your name?"

"Morning Breeze," I said, and hurried in.

At the meeting the Mayor's secretary addressed us: "Your task is to wash hands and wash feet. You will find these hands and feet in the capitalist fortresses dirtied by thick capitalist dust. You must use the hot water of the revolution to wash them. Your water must be very hot. It must be over a hundred degrees. The revolutionary water is Mao Zedong's thoughts. They will be found in the documents that you are going to study during the next nine days. You must consume the spirit of the documents. That is your spiritual food. Nourished by them, you will be strong enough to go into the capitalist fortresses to wash hands and wash feet. Then you will draw the capitalists out of the fortresses and force them to walk the Socialist Road."

In the afternoon we were asked to discuss the significance of the "Wash Hands and Wash Feet campaign." Some boy students joked, "We must use boiling water to wash them. It must be a thousand degrees. If they will not permit us to wash them, we will pour the boiling water all over them and scald them to death."

In the evening we studied by ourselves. The first document we were asked to study was entitled "Wash Hands and Wash Feet." It consisted of twenty-three points that formed the policies for the Socialist Education Movement. We had to study together in designated rooms so that the Mayor's secretary could easily check up on us. While we studied, Deng He and Yong Tian came to deliver red badges on which were written "Socialist Education Work Team" in yellow characters. Deng He sat down beside me and asked what my father did and how he had selected such a good name for me. He also asked how old I was. I told him my father was a statistician, and that he had given me this name because I was born in the early morning in summer. I told him I was seventeen.

The next morning I woke up my schoolmates at six o'clock. We all ran down to the playground where Deng He and Yong Tian were waiting. They taught us military morning exercises in which we had to jump a lot. Then they ran us in formation around the town. Breakfast was a bread roll, a boiled egg, and rice porridge. I ate less than half the bowl of the rice porridge because I was not used to eating in such a hurry.

At eight, we filled the auditorium. Deng He was on the stage. He led us in a revolutionary song, "We Are a Family of Poor Peasants." After we sang for about twenty minutes, the Mayor's secretary brought a young skinny man in dirty black work clothes onto the stage.

"Comrades!" the skinny man shrieked in a strong northern accent. "I come here to teach you how to use hot water to wash the newly-born capitalists in the countryside." His first sentence made all of us laugh because, with his accent, the words "hot water" sounded more like the words for "fresh excrement," and the word "capitalists" sounded more like "myself." He pounded his fist on the table. This stopped our laughter. He went on to say, "Thus, we can make the water hotter. They are afraid of our proletarian iron fists. We musn't be polite!" The words made us laugh again because, with his accent, he seemed to be saying, "They are afraid of our proletarian iron heads. We musn't cough at them." Just at that moment he accidently sneezed a big sneeze.

The next morning we were taken out by the Mayor's secretary to see a "Class Struggle Exhibition." The exhibits contained many old coins, old silk robes, and gold basins. The guide told us that all the old things had been confiscated from landlords and capitalists. "They keep these things because they have nostalgia for their lost past," he said. "They will never stop trying to restore their lost paradise."

On the fourth morning we were asked to watch a political movie titled, "The Vietnamese Are Our Lip and Tooth Friends." It showed how the North Vietnamese were resisting the imperialists. As the movie started, these lines appeared on the screen: "Now the imperialists are invading Vietnam. At the same time they are cooperating with the class enemies in our country. The class enemies who daydream of taking advantage of the Cultural Revolution to overthrow our government. We must watch out."

Suansuan nudged me and whispered in my ear, "What nonsense."

The fifth day we listened to "poor family histories." Two peasant women were on the stage. One carried a baby in her arms. When she moved the microphone close to begin speaking, the baby cried. She quickly unbuttoned her blouse and pulled out her breast. We bent our heads as low as we could, embarrassed to see her nakedness. The woman told us that her father and grandfather had worked all their lives for a landlord. The landlord was cruel, and he made them eat leftovers.

The other woman said her mother had been a capitalist's housekeeper for twenty years, but was fired because she accidentally lost one of the family's socks. She lost it in the river where she washed the laundry. Both women ended their speeches with the same shouts: "Down with the landlord class! Down with the capitalists! Never forget class bitterness! Never forget to take revenge on the class enemies!"

The remaining days we made hundreds of posters of Chairman Mao's sayings. "Choose the saying from Chairman Mao that can solve your problem," the Mayor's secretary said. "Chairman Mao is truth. His thoughts can solve all of your problems. Chairman Mao's quotations are the doctor's prescriptions that can cure diseases of the mind. Set the doctor beside your pillow so you can see him every morning and every evening. In this way you will never be sick with bourgeois diseases."

For our posters, most of us chose the quotation, "We are friends, we come from different provinces, we must help each other." Suansuan wrote a quotation from the ancient Chinese philosopher, Lao Zi: "The Heavenly Father sends everyone to earth as king, so long as he is diligent in learning, thinking and acting."

I asked her: "Why do you write Lao Zi's quotation instead of Chairman Mao's?"

She grinned and said: "Chairman Mao once quoted this in his speech. Now I am quoting from his speech."

I usually stayed up late at night to read and think. Before I went to bed, I always took a shower in the public bathroom outside the building. Many nights I met Deng He, who was walking alone. He always greeted me, "Hello, Little Devil. How are you this evening?"

"I'm fine, thank you," I would answer.

On the ninth evening Deng He organized a farewell party for us. He asked each school to perform one or two skits at the party. Our school comedian, Xian Hui, offered to represent our school.

The auditorium now became our theater with green curtains hung on the stage. Deng He performed first, singing a revolutionary song, "A Lamp Shines in Chairman Mao's Window." He had a good voice and stage presence, and he was handsome. Comrade Yong was next. He demonstrated military boxing. Then it was our school's turn.

20

When the curtain opened, Xian Hui was standing with her back to us. There was no music. She wore a deep brown robe. Her hair was in a bun tied with a large red ribbon. Before we realized what was going to happen, she spun around and gave a big smile. Her almond eyes and two protruding front teeth made her smile great fun, and all the audience laughed. She then quit smiling and bowed, announcing her show. Her voice was a high-pitched falsetto. "An Egg," she said.

Stepping this way and that with small light steps, she opened and closed her hands like flowers. A delicate wail arose from her hands, from small pieces of bamboo that she pressed together and then released. She sang to the accompaniment of music: "In Village Wang lives Fortune Wang. He is famous for being lazy. And famous for good luck. One day he strolls out and finds an egg on the road. 'Thank the Fortune Buddha,' he says, and picks it up. He sets the egg in his palm and gazes at it. He gazes hard at it, and sees a wonder. The egg can be hatched into a chicken, a chicken will lay more eggs. The eggs can be hatched into more chickens, the chickens will lay still more eggs. He says, 'I will sell the eggs to buy a little lamb. The little lamb will grow into a big lamb. I will sell the big lamb to buy a little cow. The little cow will grow into a big cow. I will sell the big cow to buy a little horse. The little horse will grow into a big horse. I will ride the big horse to visit a rich woman. I will ask her to marry me, and then, I Fortune Wang, will be Rich Wang.' Suddenly he tripped and slipped. His egg fell and broke."

Xian Hui stopped singing. The music stopped. She faked a big cry, and threw herself to the ground. The curtain dropped. Our Xian Hui earned a storm of applause.

It was late in the evening after I took a shower and

21

started back. Deng He met me on the way. "How nice to see you, Little Devil," he said, and took my hand. "Xian Hui from your school is a fine actress. But remember, never give that performance again. It was written by a rightist who used "An Egg" to attack The People's Commune established by Chairman Mao in 1958. The author meant to say that The People's Commune is an empty dream that ends up as a broken egg."

I was upset to hear that. I looked at the moon. It was a full moon, reminding me that this was the middle of July, the time I should have been taking the National Examination for College Entrance. Two months had passed since the Cultural Revolution began, two months that would never come to me again. Did the moon know what had happened here on earth?

"Little Devil, I feel sad because you are leaving. When can I see you again?" His voice was soft. I turned to look at him, trying to make sure what he said. "See my white shirt. There are so many spots here and there that make it a black shirt." I turned to watch the moon again. A breeze stirred; it was gentle and cool. "Breeze," he exclaimed. "Morning Breeze. Beautiful! You are beautiful. You are the most beautiful girl I've ever known. Will you write to me? Please write to me."

I was so surprised that I rushed to my room without answering.

Lying on my bed, I couldn't sleep, my heart beat very fast. I heard the clock chime one. I tried harder to sleep. Then I heard the clock chime two, then three, then four, and then I got up to pack. A steamboat would carry us across the river at five o'clock, and trucks would take us to the mountain villages, to the communes. My commune was to be the Three Stars Commune, thirty miles away.

At the pier I saw Deng He. I pretended I didn't notice him, and walked onto the boat. When the boat started off, all the students waved to him and called goodbye. I covered my face with my straw hat.

I waved until I couldn't see them anymore.

CHAPTER 3

In the Bandit Village

土 壩 庄

The young peasant guide and I walked silently from one bare field to another in the late, hot afternoon. The sun was scorching, the fields of wheat stubble looked extremely vast, and I felt very small. The guide had met me at the Three Stars Commune office, and told me I was being sent to a bandit village, the Three Stars Village. After we crossed the fifth field the Three Stars Village came into view—thatched-roof houses scattered randomly about, shabby and low. We entered the village, where an old lady of about seventy was standing by a door. "She is your hostess," the guide told me. "She is Grandma Li."

I entered Grandma Li's house where two older men politely received me. These were Monitor Ding and the Political Commissar. "Welcome to our Educational Work Team," they said and shook my hand.

"Our work team has now grown to twelve members,"

the Political Commissar told me with a smile.

Monitor Ding was a skinny man with a serious face. He wore a clean, faded blue shirt, like any peasant leader. The Political Commissar was short, round and smiling. Like an intellectual, he wore two pens in his white shirt pocket. As we drank tea, Monitor Ding told me that ninety-five percent of the villagers were bandits before the revolution. They had led the Three Stars Bandit Uprising in 1950, in an attempt to drive out the Communists. That was why this commune was called the Three Stars.

The Political Commissar tried to encourage me, "Don't be afraid," he said, "you will do a good job. We will support you. All the comrades in this work team will support you."

"Where are they?" I asked.

"They are in different villages, just miles away," Monitor Ding said.

"Are there any students in the team?" I asked the Political Commissar.

"No," he said. "They are factory workers, retired soldiers, and clerks, but they are very nice. They have been in this commune for over a month. They have experience in how to wash hands and wash feet. They will help you."

Grandma Li's house had two rooms, and mine was a small, neat one at the back. The earthen floor was clean. There was a double bed, a desk and a new wooden bucket—my toilet. In the mud wall behind the bed I saw a little bamboo door. I opened it: a huge black mountain started almost from the doorstep, blocking the sky. Frightened, I slammed the door shut. Just then, Grandma Li called me to dinner.

There were bowls of wheat porridge and pickled cucumbers on the table by her bed. We sat down and ate. Grandma

Li seemed not to want to talk to me. After dinner, she brought me a basin of warm water and a fresh towel. I washed my dusty face, which made the water muddy. She took the same water and began to wash herself with it.

"Oh, no, Grandma Li!" I said: "Don't use it, I will warm you some clean water."

She ignored me. And then when she finished, she said, "We have only one well. It's far behind the mountain, and we don't have enough firewood for cooking, so we don't often have warm water."

I was touched by this and I offered, "Grandma Li, I will carry water for you every day."

I took five yuan from my pocket and insisted she use it to buy some firewood. Grandma Li refused, saying she was paid by the Commune for taking care of me. But she gradually grew talkative and friendly, and she saw me to bed that night.

The next morning I got up early, went to the well, and carried water home. After breakfast, Monitor Ding and the Political Commissar arrived.

"We have come here to hold a village meeting," they said, "to show you how to wash hands and wash feet. This village remains a closed bottle because its former team leader, Liu Zhenwen, is a stubborn element. We must start political surgery on him. Chairman Mao teaches us: 'Use scissors to cut a sparrow, beginning with the head.'"

When Monitor Ding blew his whistle, all the villagers dragged themselves into the yard—old and young, men and women, children and babies. They found space and sat down on the grass. Monitor Ding stood before them and declared in a loud voice, "Comrades, it is high time for you to confess your crimes. We have checked on every one of you and discovered the serious crimes you have committed. There is no way for you to escape. I urge you to confess right now, to wash hands and wash feet by yourselves. If you fail to confess, we will wash them for you. But by then, don't complain if the water is too hot. Revolution accepts no excuse and has no mercy. Believe it!" The villagers were silent.

A man finally stood up, walked towards me, and said, "I want to confess my crime to you." I quickly stood up and looked at Monitor Ding. He nodded permission. I went with the man out of the yard.

Sitting in a field, he said: "My name is Liu Zhenwen."

"Liu Zhenwen, the former leader?" I asked.

"Yes, I used to be."

"What are you going to tell me about?" I opened my notebook.

"I am a criminal. In 1958 I helped carry out the Deep-Plough-Land Movement. It brought death to my people. Half of them died of hunger. This movement called for digging the fields two meters deep, and burying seeds there. The following year nothing grew. My people had to eat grass, tree bark, leaves, and mud."

He paused. "Grandma Li's three children died in one day. They were buried in one grave. Blind Grandpa Zhou's two sons died too." He paused again. "Peasants called me father, because I was a village leader, but I could only watch them die at my feet." He looked away.

"Mr. Liu is a good man, I'm sure," I immediately decided, and put my notebook aside. I remembered the Deep-Plough-Land campaign. It was part of the People's Commune movement launched in 1958 by Chairman Mao. The goal was to bring more crops from the land. I was ten years old then, in grade school. All the teachers talked about the campaign, telling us "the two-meter-deep land will grow peanuts as big as potatoes, and cotton bolls as big as a baby's round face." And there was a Saturday afternoon. After the music teacher taught us a song, "The Deep-Plough-Land Movement Is Excellent," we hurried to have supper, then followed him to a village to "entertain" the villagers. "They are carrying out Chairman Mao's campaign," the teacher instructed us. That was a cold winter night. The mountain wind blew, making a sound like animals screaming. In the fields I saw a great many political slogans on paper flags hanging in the trees. And under the kerosene lamps I saw the villagers digging into the ground. The holes were so deep I was worried I might fall in.

The next year one-third of my classmates died of hunger. As a boarding student then, I remembered how for many months each of my meals had been just three little boiled yams.

Mr. Liu began to puff on his pipe.

"Did any village leader reject the Deep-Plough-Land Movement?" I asked.

"Yes, but they were beaten to death. The village leader of the No. Two Team Village was beaten for three days."

"Who beat them?"

"People from other villages."

I had heard of that, too, when I was ten. Mr. Liu was telling the truth. Then I asked him, "Are ninety-five percent of the villagers here bandits?"

"No," he was sure.

"Then how did the commune get the name, the Three Stars?"

"It is because of a pavilion not far from here. It is shaped like a triangle. Our people call a triangle 'three stars.'"

"But I heard that there'd been a reactionary uprising called the 'Three Stars.'"

He shook his head and told me that it was a made-up story.

The next morning I reported to Monitor Ding and the Political Commissar that Mr. Liu was innocent. But the monitor said, "He is a blatant class enemy! He seized on the small shortcomings in the Deep-Plough-Land Movement to attack the People's Commune Movement launched by Chairman Mao." They both said, "You mustn't be so naive."

Two weeks passed. Monitor Ding and the Political Commissar assigned me many documents to study and constantly reminded me that I must try to raise my political consciousness. I read them during the day at Grandma Li's house. Sometimes I held a meeting to read aloud the documents to the villagers. But I spent most of my evenings visiting the peasants after they returned from the fields. They seemed friendly to me, and called me Little Comrade. They came to visit me too, at Li's house, to "confess" their "crimes." One villager "confessed" that he had taken home an old broom that belonged to the village. A woman confessed that she had taken some dry peas from the fields and put them into her own pockets. A young boy confessed that he had said that Marshal Lin Biao's eyebrows looked like two worms. "My crime is most serious because I said such a bad thing about a government leader," he said.

Blind Grandpa Zhou lived at the end of the village with his aged wife. When I learned the villagers carried water for the couple by turn, I joined in. Besides, I often helped them with sewing and mending.

At night, at Grandma Li's there were many mosquitoes. While reading, I had to wear long-sleeved shirts and thick pants to protect myself. This made me sweat. To save firewood, I washed myself with cold water, and discovered that the water from the well was icy cold even in summer.

Monitor Ding and the Political Commissar often dropped in to see me. They seemed satisfied with my work, saying I had opened the "closed bottle" since so many villagers had confessed. The Political Commissar once joked with me, "Your water is really hot." They also told me they had moved into a nearby village office three li away, and asked me to report my work to them at any time.

The villagers seemed to enjoy chatting with me while I was eating supper. They sat on the floor or on Grandma Li's bed. They told me they seldom went to see a doctor. When they got sick, they warmed their feet in hot water, and, if very ill, fasted for a whole day. "It really works," they declared. When one of their children got sick, they would say "the child is not pretty."

I liked the village girls very much. They were simple, honest and sweet. They were curious about my clothes. I let them open my suitcase to look through my clothes and try them on. One day they saw my sanitary napkins, and asked what they were for. "For my period," I said.

"What? You also have a period? We thought only country girls had that thing."

Red was their favorite color. "Why do all of you like the same color?" I asked one day.

"It chases ghosts away."

"Where are the ghosts?"

"Everywhere." Then they showed their red paper wallets to me. "You see, we use red paper to make wallets so we won't meet thieves and never lose money." They opened their wallets and I found none had more than a few coins.

One day a letter came from Deng He. My heart beat fast. He wrote:

Dear Little Devil,
    I have been wondering how things are going with

you. You must be busy getting yourself adjusted to new conditions, just as I did when I came to the commune. It took me three weeks to adjust.

May I tell you something more about myself? I was born in 1946, in Yi Bing. It is a handsome city, where three rivers meet, the Lin Jiang, Min Jiang, and Jialing Jiang. The waters of the Lin Jiang and Jialing Jiang are so clear you can see the sand on the bottom, and from far away they look like emerald-colored silk ribbons. Min Jiang flows from the Yellow River so it is always yellow. My home is on the banks of the river. Day and night I can hear the roaring of the waters. I like watching the many white-sailed boats that pass by and I often hear the chanting of the trackers. My father, who died many years ago, was a writer. My mother is a painter in water colors. As a child I often sat with mother in front of the house, under the willows, and painted the scenery. I have three brothers, all of whom are now military commanders. I am the youngest in the family, and my mother loves me best.

The day I left home for the military academy was my eighteenth birthday. Mother walked with me all the way to the door of the train. As the train started to move she stood there alone on the platform for a long long time. I knew she was crying. Ever since, I've come to feel that the most painful thing in life is to have to say goodbye. So, now when I return home I always tell mother not to give me any kind of send-off when I leave again. I myself never give anyone a send-off either. I'm afraid to say goodbye.

But that day you went away I did want to see you off. That morning I walked back and forth along the dock, hoping I'd be able to see you again . . .

My home is only 200 li away from yours. I wish so much you could come to visit me there someday.

Today I am writing to you, alone in my room. It is late in the evening. Today is my twentieth birthday. I am so happy to be able to write you. I miss you very much. The first time I saw you, I had an unexplainable feeling about you. Please be kind enough to write to me. I am waiting for your letter.

Deng He

In the envelope I found a few stamps. He must have thought that I had no money to buy stamps.

I wrote to him:

Dear Comrade Deng,

Thank you very much for your letter. My village is in the mountains and has ninety-six villagers. They are kind to me, although they know I am a student. I have no idea how they found out I am a student. Maybe it is because of something that happened on the third day after my arrival. I was walking along a narrow road by a flooded rice paddy. The road was wet and slippery, and several times I nearly slid into the water. It amused me and made me laugh out loud. When I reported this incident to my monitor and the Political Commissar, they instructed me not to laugh in front of the villagers, because I am not a student any more but in the ranks of revolutionary cadres. And a revolutionary cadre must be very serious.

I will say goodbye to you now.

Little Devil

He wrote me again in a week, and gave more details about his family. His grandfather had been a magistrate during the Qin Dynasty and had left a great many valuable books, including sets and sets of original Tang Dynasty and Song Dynasty poems, some Yuan Dynasty plays, and some Qin Dynasty novels. Deng He's father had started writing at seven. He had won recognition for his poetry and short stories.

After reading this second letter, I thought about his family, an intellectual family, and wondered how they had managed to get positions in the military for all their children. Such positions led to a comfortable life, political preference, and other special treatment. He must have been born into a high-ranking official's family, I concluded, and put his letter at the bottom of my valise. I did not like the children of high-ranking officials. Too often they were spoiled.

After supper, I decided to visit Mr. Liu's home. I was determined to prove that Mr. Liu was not a class enemy but a good man. Standing outside his window, I saw both he and his wife reading a small book by the light of an oil lamp. The book cover was red, a certain sign that it was one of Chairman Mao's works. They were reading intently. I decided not to disturb them and went on to visit neighbor Zhen's home.

I was shocked to find Mr. and Mrs. Zhen, his mother, and their five sons sitting on the earthen floor naked except for undershorts. Mrs. Zhen explained to me that they didn't have enough clothes to wear. They saved the few they had for going into the village. She also told me that they didn't have enough rice bowls for all to eat at the same time, and so she and her mother-in-law had to eat after the others had finished.

That night I tossed in my bed, feeling guilty. For seventeen years I had never given the peasants a thought. Those who produced food for me had to struggle for their own survival. At about one o'clock I heard raindrops, then a downpour. Our house was leaking. Grandma Li and I got up to hunt for basins, buckets, and pots to catch the rain.

I thought of blind Grandpa Zhou and rushed to his house.

His door was open and I saw Mr. Liu inside, helping Mrs. Zhou sweep the rain water from the floor. In one corner stood blind Grandpa Zhou on crutches. The water seemed under control.

On my way back in the dim light I saw almost every family fighting the rain. I rushed to the village office to get Monitor Ding and the Political Commissar. I banged and kicked at the door, and called, "Get up, get up!"

When they opened the door I pulled them out, shouting, "Come quick! It's a tragedy! We must do something!" They finally understood what I wanted and they smiled. Monitor Ding asked, "You walked all this way in the rain? It is already two o'clock in the morning!" Then they accompanied me home. The Political Commissar warned, "Don't walk alone at night anymore. This is a bandit area."

When morning came, I called an emergency meeting and organized a group of young peasants to repair the leaking houses. Many families donated bamboo, wood, and wheat stalks. We worked hard, and before evening, had repaired all the roofs.

Monitor Ding and the Political Commissar praised me highly. They recommended me to the Ganyang city government as an "Advanced Revolutionary Cadre," and nominated me for membership in the Communist Party. "You are a qualified Communist because you do things according to our great leader Chairman Mao's teaching: 'Serve the people with your heart and soul.'" As a result, the Ganyang city government held a meeting of four-hundred people to honor me. Every student who was a work team member was present, and, as an award, the Mayor gave me a handsome notebook. I did not understand, though, why they should nominate me to become a

Communist Party member. After all, the houses I'd helped repair belonged to "bandits." Or, didn't they really believe they were bandits either?

On the sixth week a new policy came down from Beijing—from Chairman Mao. It was announced that all students must immediately return to school. Monitor Ding and the Political Commissar came to see me. They looked sad. They held my hands in theirs, and silently sat beside me for a long time.

"Why does Chairman Mao send us back to school in such a hurry?" I asked.

"There is something urgent," the Political Commissar answered. "Chairman Mao announced the policy in Shanghai last night. The policy states that to send the Educational Work Teams to the countryside is wrong."

"You mean to wash hands and wash feet is not correct?" I asked.

They didn't answer. Monitor Ding merely said, "Our work team is going to be dismissed next week."

That night I wrote to Deng He, giving him my school address. Then I packed. I was to leave early next morning. Grandma Li shed tears as she saw me to bed.

After an early breakfast I left two cakes of scented soap I had brought with me on Grandmother Li's bed, and I opened the door. To my great surprise, I saw the yard was packed solidly with villagers. They were standing in complete silence, waiting to see me. Emotion overcame me. Many were crying. Grandpa Zhou touched my face with his hand and said, "I hate that my eyes can't see you."

The villagers walked with me down to the river. No one talked. Grandpa Zhou, on his crutch, walked shoulder to shoulder with me.

Mr. Liu carried my bags onto the boat. Holding my

hands in his own, he said, "My people will remember you."

The ferryman lifted his oar and began paddling. As the boat slid away from the riverbank, a long, low cry rose from the villagers. I caught my breath and waved to them. I waved until I couldn't see them anymore.

CHAPTER 4

Ransacking a Capitalist's Fortress

抄 家

The atmosphere at school was cold; nobody welcomed us. We were asked to sit in our old classroom on benches arranged in a circle. The Woman Hero stood in the center. "Comrades," she announced, raising her arm as if she were a high party official. On her arm there was a Red Guard arm band. "Today I have scheduled all of you to read Chairman Mao's *Quotations*." A male Red Guard carrying a basket full of little red books stood up and began passing them out to us.

Suansuan huddled in the corner as usual, deep in her own thoughts. When the Red Guard handed her a little red book, she didn't seem to notice. I looked around, trying to find Meimei. All the Black Sorts kept their heads lowered and wore grief on their faces. I could not find Meimei.

"Open your book to page 352. Find the second paragraph and read out loud," the Woman Hero ordered. Immediately, all the Red Guards began to chant in rhythm, "Imperialists and all reactionaries are paper tigers. The relationship between the proletarian class and the capitalist class is like a white knife going through a body, then becoming a red knife."

Next, the Woman Hero ordered us to turn to another page. That morning she ordered over twenty quotations read.

During a break I asked Suansuan about Meimei. "Is she sick?"

"I don't know."

"Shall we go to see her this afternoon?"

"I don't know."

"What's wrong with you Suansuan? Did I offend you?"

"I don't know."

"You must tell me why you treat me like that."

"You're an opportunist." She walked away.

I was stunned, and hurt. I quickly realized Suansuan must have thought I helped repair the villagers' houses to show off and earn political credits so I could join the Communist Party and become a Party official, like the Woman Hero.

She misunderstood me, but I didn't want to try to explain. No one had ever called me an opportunist before. To me that was the dirtiest word in the language. I thought of Meimei. Meimei was always kind. She would never call me an opportunist. Oh, how I missed her! How I missed the days when we played ping-pong and fished together. Meimei was such fun.

That afternoon, as soon as class was dismissed, I ran all the way to Meimei's house.

The house had been painted bright red. A big sign propped up at the front garden gate read: "East Commune

Office." I knocked on the door and asked about my friend. The commune official said, "She is dead."

"Excuse me?"

The official looked straight at me. "She is dead. She committed suicide."

I screamed.

He slowly lit a cigar, looked toward the river, and said, "She jumped into Snake River. Her mother buried her and has gone South." He turned, entered the house, and shut the door.

Meimei is dead. My best friend, Meimei, dead. I couldn't believe it. I walked down to Snake River and sat by the bank till dark.

When I came home, I didn't find my parents. They were in low spirits these days. I decided not to tell them about Meimei.

I lay down, and turned off the lights. The house was very quiet. The world seemed dead and I felt I was dead.

Each day now seemed like a year, and I was all alone. Every evening I went for a long walk. The world was dark and had left me alone with my shadow.

I hated school. I hated everything there. I hated the Woman Hero. They had killed Meimei. Yet I still had to go there to read Chairman Mao's *Quotations*. It was the demand of the revolutionary times.

The Woman Hero sometimes went to the Cowshed, recently set up at No. Two High School, to supervise our teachers. The Cowshed was a place of internment where the teachers were "re-educated" and humiliated. All the teachers were being called "Cow Monsters" and "Snake Demons," because they had supported the bourgeois educational system and methods.

One evening I passed by the house of Teacher Bo. He had been my beloved teacher of Chinese literature for three years

40

and I thought very highly of him. His wife motioned me to come to the door.

"Teacher Bo is very ill," she told me in a low voice.

"What's the matter?"

"He jumped from the second floor of the Cowshed. His back is injured."

"What made him do that?"

"They accused him of being a counterrevolutionary because of a joke he told in your class. It was about a coffin shop."

I remembered that joke. He told it last summer in an afternoon class when we were suffering from the heat. "One day," he said, "I saw a long line in front of a shop. I thought something wonderful must be sold there, so I joined the line. When my turn came, I discovered they were selling coffins."

Teacher Bo often told such jokes, but now, Mrs. Bo said, he had been been accused of using the joke to attack the People's Commune created by Chairman Mao in 1958—a time when many people died of hunger.

She took me to the bed where teacher Bo lay. His eyes were closed, his face deathly pale.

Mrs. Bo told me he had been in the hospital for two weeks, but no nurse was allowed to take care of him. The wounds on his back had become infected and grew worms. The student standing guard had not even allowed her to bring him good food. "One day when the guard discovered I had brought him an egg roll," Mrs. Bo said, "she snatched it and threw it out the window."

"Who is the guard?" I asked.

"Chen Ziling, the Woman Hero."

This is hell, I thought all the way home.

The next morning in school, a Red Guard ordered me

to go to the principal's office. I knocked at the door and entered. The Woman Hero sat in the principal's chair.

"You've got a task," she said, giving me a smirk. "Tomorrow morning at seven come here to lead students to ransack a capitalist's house." I didn't answer, and she continued, "Our great leader Chairman Mao has just issued a new policy today—the Sixteen Points, which you will find in today's newspaper. The policy calls on us to start a new drive to destroy the "Four Olds"—old culture, old customs, old traditions and the old feudal system. Have you heard that Beijing Red Guards and Shanghai Red Guards are burning temples and ransacking houses of the capitalists? It is the revolutionary storm. Now we will start a storm here."

Before I could respond she handed me a red arm band, on which was written: "Red Guard Out-Circle."

"What does that mean?" I asked.

"It means you are accepted as a member of the Red Guard Out-Circle."

"What is an out-circle?"

"A subordinate organization of the Red Guard Organization."

"Sounds funny, doesn't it?"

"Nothing is funny!"

"I mean who ever heard of such a funny name for an organization?"

"Stop talking to me like that! Nothing in revolutionary times is funny. The relation between an Out-Circle and a Red Guard is like the relationship between the Communist Party Youth League and the Communist Party. Before joining the Communist Party you have to be accepted in the Youth League, right? The Youth League is the Out-Circle of the Party. Let me remind you, you're still a member of the Youth League and I'm the League's leader, and the leader of the Red Guards. All orders of the revolutionary organizations must be obeyed."

Then she said, "Tomorrow come to school early to ransack Zhou Bin Yun's house. He is a capitalist who lives at 237 South Road, Tai Ping District." Then she asked me to leave.

I was furious. Walking out, I clenched my fists and said to myself, "I must stop her. I must fight her. I must bring her down!"

I slept badly that night. What was the best way to fight her? I had to find it. First, I would obey her completely. Then the Red Guards would let me join their organization. I would try to establish myself in power. Only by climbing up to the same political position as she would I have a chance to defeat her.

When I arrived at school the next morning, the thirty students chosen by the Woman Hero were waiting. As I led them to the capitalist's house, two other school teams joined us. We marched together and shouted, "Down with the capitalist Zhou Bin Yun! Long Live the Red Guards! Long Live the Great Proletarian Cultural Revolution!"

It was an ordinary brick house. The door was sagging. Inside, the capitalist, a thin old man, sat on a wooden bench at the door. He looked half-starved. As soon as he saw us, he stood and bowed to us. "Welcome, Red Guard Generals." The house contained only two small rooms, a bedroom and a kitchen. There was a simple bed, a table, and an ash heap beside the stove. The students who had squeezed in rushed immediately to the ashes to dig for gold. The found nothing but chicken dung.

"Where is the gold?" one Red Guard demanded.

"I have none," the old man answered. He looked honest.

"If you refuse to show us the gold, we will kill you!" roared many of the guards. Then all the students started digging up the floor and destroying the walls. I did the same.

At noon, a smiling middle-aged woman walked into the house. She invited us to have tea next door in her yard. As we drank the tea, she called the old man a capitalist parasite, and urged us to send him to the countryside. Gradually, as she chattered on, I came to realize that the smiling woman was actually the old man's daughter-in-law, and that this was a family war. The daughter-in-law was trying to use the glorious Cultural Revolution to drive the old man out so she could take over his house.

On our way back to the school, we saw the Woman Hero with a group of Red Guards throwing household goods and books out of the apartments of various teachers. None of the teachers were at home.

The Woman Hero called to me and ordered me to take the old man to the countryside the next day.

"Why?" I asked.

"Because he is a bad capitalist."

"Who is a good capitalist then?"

"A good one must show us his gold."

"But if he doesn't have gold, how could he show it?"

"Shut up! He has gold!"

"Who saw the gold?"

"His daughter-in-law," she said with a smirk, as if she had won the argument.

I didn't want to waste another word with her. She was a witch! As I turned away she called after me, "Tomorrow morning, get to school before seven to take him to the coun- tryside. I will arrange for eight students to go with you."

All night I argued with myself. I wanted to fight the Woman Hero at once. But at last I calmed down. I kept telling myself:

You've got to obey her! That's the only way to get into the Red Guards; the only way to carry out the plan.

I got up at six and went to the school. It was very windy that morning. I wore two sweaters and a jacket, although it was only early September. The eight students the Woman Hero had selected were young, about fourteen years old.

The old man was standing at his door. Beside him were two baskets filled with his clothes, cooking wok, kettle, and pickle pot. He held a bamboo pole in one hand. He began to tie his baskets to the pole as we neared the house. He lifted it to his shoulders, and asked me, "Shall I go now?"

"I don't know where we're to go," I admitted, feeling sad for him.

"I know," the old man answered, "They told me to go to my relatives' village."

We followed him out to the mud road, then along a narrower road, then up a steep, curving mountain path. He walked fast, and we had to run to keep up with him. He told us it was 30 miles to the village, and would take us at least fifteen hours to get there.

I began to sweat, and removed my jacket. The other students did too. Later we took off our sweaters. Before noon, my stomach began to rumble. I felt hungry, then very hungry, then not hungry at all, but exhausted.

"Can we take a rest?" a student asked me.

"No." I knew that once we sat down we would not stand up again. We were too tired to rest.

We walked slower and slower and fell far behind the "capitalist." Now and then, he stopped and waited for us.

By the late afternoon we were dead-tired. Nobody talked. We didn't even have the strength to speak.

Suddenly the old man began dancing. He stumbled back and forth like a drunk, then curved his legs to imitate a duck's walk, while he swung his two baskets high into the air and hummed a folk melody, then he started singing:

> A plump girl visits her mother at night. In a
> hurry she picks up a pillow and puts it on her
> back instead of her baby. Passing through a
> pumpkin field, she slips and falls. She loses
> her pillow and picks up a pumpkin instead.
> The foolish plump girl carries no baby but
> a pumpkin to see her mother.

We started laughing. We laughed and walked, and finally arrived in the village. It was pitch dark. All the villagers came out to receive the old man. Some called him "grandpa," some called him "uncle." The little ones hugged his legs and cheered. The old man smiled.

We were invited to have dinner with him, a delicious yam and pork soup. After dinner, we were very tired, so the old man and his relatives took us to the village inn.

The innkeeper arranged for the nine of us students to sleep in one room, boys on the left side, girls on the right.

When I took off my shoes and socks I found my feet were covered with bloody blisters. I lay down and heard the sobs of the boys and girls. Their feet hurt too, I knew.

The next morning we could not walk. The innkeeper felt sorry for us, so he stopped three trucks, which were transporting sugar cane to the city, and asked the drivers to take us home.

I rested at home for three days. By the fourth day I was able to get on my feet again and went back to school. There they told me a young man from the military had come to see me. His name was Deng He.

CHAPTER 5

Revolutionary Storms

革命风暴

Hundreds of Red Guards—university students from Beijing, Shanghai, and Tianjin—came to our city, declaring Chairman Mao had told them to spread the revolution to their home places. They offered free lectures in the streets in the evenings, saying that the Cultural Revolution was a contest of strength between the proletarian class and the capitalist class. This revolution was to deal with the most dangerous enemies in our country. They were capitalist roaders because they were within the Communist party, hiding under the Marxist cloak, but opposed to Marxism.

Nobody understood exactly how the new enemies had wrapped themselves in the red flag of our glorious Communist Party and now had suddenly revealed themselves. To try to understand all this I started to attend the lectures held near my home. To my great surprise, I heard people shouting "Bombard the municipal government and burn down the City Hall!"

At another evening lecture, a university Red Guard called out to the audience, "Let's go to the City Hall to take the revolution to the mayor, because he is the biggest capitalist roader in the city." At this, the audience shouted agreement and rushed with the university Red Guards to the City Hall. I followed and, caught up in the excitement of the moment, also shouted the slogans led by the university Red Guards. "Down with the capitalist roaders! Liberate Sichuan! Down with the mayor! Liberate the city people!" When we arrived at the City Hall, we found all the doors shut. Lights shone from only a few windows. The university Red Guards told us to sit surrounding the building. They shouted, "Come out! Xiu Hongkun! If you don't raise your two hands in surrender to us, you will die!" A student at my left told me, "To sit around a building this way is called a revolutionary sit-down demonstration."

We sat on the ground in the dew. The university Red Guards kept telling us, "Stay to the end, victory will be ours!" They led us in chanting, "Arrest the Mayor, Xiu Hongkun! Execute the Mayor, Xiu Hongkun! Cut the Mayor into pieces and throw the pieces to dogs!"

The doors slowly opened, and the Mayor's secretary came out. But before he could open his mouth, the university Red Guards shouted, "Down with the running dog of a Mayor! Smash the running dog! Execute the running dog! Cut him into a thousand pieces!" He retreated indoors, slowly, as if he were dragging a great weight. Then the university Red Guards began beating on the doors, yelling, "Come out, Xiu Hongkun! If you don't come out in one minute we'll break down the doors and smash the windows and kidnap you!"

The Mayor himself finally appeared. As he approached us he shouted, "Down with Mayor Xiu Hongkun! Down with the capitalist roader, Xiu Hongkun!" This sounded so foolish we burst into laughter. He bowed low to us, said, "Good evening, Red Guard Generals. I admire you very much in carrying out our great leader Chairman Mao's revolutionary policies and coming to help me. You are one hundred percent right. I am a capitalist roader. I have committed unforgivable crimes. I will confess them before all the citizens. Thank you very much."

The mayor then raised his left hand, looked at his watch, and said, "I guess, first of all, I should take you to a restaurant for a meal. You see, it is nearly midnight, you've been here for two hours. I can't let you carry out the Cultural Revolution on empty stomachs."

Hearing this, two university Red Guards jumped up to the platform and ordered, "Go! Lead the way." Everybody stood up and followed them to the restaurant. I went home.

Within a week, the university Red Guards had released all the teachers from the cowsheds and jails, telling them that they were "small potatoes," and that the Cultural Revolution wanted the "big potatoes" who were leaders in the Communist Party.

One Beijing Red Guard, Mr. Xiong, was a former schoolmate of mine. He often visited the apartment of Teacher Wei, our math teacher, and he began holding lectures in the teacher's apartment. Once he even gave a lecture in Wei's bedroom, half lying on the bed, a cigar in his mouth. Teacher Wei was proud of his former student. He served tea and candies enthusiastically whenever such a lecture was held in his apartment. Many other teachers invited this former student for lunch or dinner. They were grateful to him because he was among the Red Guards who had released them from the cowsheds.

Xiong told me he had seen Chairman Mao five times. "Chairman Mao, The Old Man, is in good health. That is our good luck. You see, The Old Man is the big tree who supports us, bringing us cool shade in summer and protecting us from the cold winter. Let's wish The Old Man a long, long life."

"Do all the Beijing Red Guards call Chairman Mao The Old Man?" I asked.

"Yes. That is most respectful. Don't you call your grandfather 'Old Man' because you respect him?" he explained.

"Have you ever seen comrade Jiang Qing?" another student from our school asked. "Is she in good health? We wish her good health since she is Chairman Mao's wife."

"Yes, she is in good health, too. She accompanies The Old Man when he appears before us on the Tiananmen balcony. She waves to us and calls us, 'Red Guard Generals.' She herself dresses like a Red Guard, in a green uniform with a red arm band. You know, she has revised eight old operas into revolutionary operas for the Cultural Revolution. In Beijing people call her the 'Flag-Bearer' of the Cultural Revolution."

"Can you give us a more specific idea about Chairman Mao's strategy for the Cultural Revolution?" a teacher asked.

"To get rid of all the capitalist roaders throughout China.

"How many capitalist roaders are there?" I asked.

"Thousands and thousands. Almost every Communist Party leader in a provincial government, city government, county government, in school leadership and work unit leadership are capitalist roaders."

"How can we get rid of them all?"

"It's going to be a huge job. That's why The Old Man

launched the Cultural Revolution, the greatest revolution ever in Chinese history. You know, it's such a difficult job that even The Old Man himself doesn't quite know if the revolution will succeed or fail. He might have to return to the Jinggangshan Mountains where he started the peasant uprising in 1928, to re-liberate China."

"Is the situation so dangerous?" another teacher asked.

"Yes, we must all follow Chairman Mao to the Jinggangshan Mountains when he calls on us. We must prepare to give our lives at any moment. Revolution needs blood, and may require other great sacrifices too. I am prepared. If the revolution needs my head I will cut it off. For me it will be just like taking off my hat."

Teacher Wei never forgot to invite me to his dinners with Xiong. He was fond of me, even though in math I was not at the top of my class. As a matter of fact, the first year in high school I was a bit afraid of him. He had a long, serious face and never joked with the students. He was over forty, and single. Perhaps his serious appearance scared away women, I thought. But he taught well.

In the streets, the university Red Guards set up a lot of revolutionary stations where they read the newspapers through loudspeakers, distributed pamphlets and maps, and urged people to prepare to follow Chairman Mao to the Jinggangshan Mountains. Constantly they broadcast an old revolutionary song:

> Off with my head if I leave the truth behind;
> We will wake up our people to carry the
> Revolution through to the end.

Everyone talked about the Cultural Revolution now. When people met, instead of saying hello or mentioning the weather, they asked, "What have you heard from the revolutionary stations?" My parents frequently brought pamphlets home, and each time they read them, they would began to argue. "The Cultural Revolution is a kid's game," my mother stated.

"No," my father said, "It is Chairman Mao's strategy for re-liberating China."

"In my opinion, it is a game thought up by someone who has nothing better to do than make trouble."

"You should go listen to the free lectures so that you can understand the great significance of the Cultural Revolution."

"I would rather sleep than go see that kid's game. I'm busy enough with my own affairs," my mother said.

"But they are from Beijing, from Chairman Mao."

"If they said they were from heaven, you would also believe them. Why don't you draw a lesson from the Anti-Rightist Movement of 1957, when all the clever men joined that game of criticizing the Party's policies? They were labeled rightists and were thrown into jail. Remember the old philosophy: 'Be a silent snake rather than a singing bird.' Stay at home, keep your mouth and ears shut and no trouble will come to you."

In the streets a great many people could be seen—husbands and wives, fathers and sons—pointing fingers at each other's noses and arguing. The Cultural Revolution had affected every family.

Our school became a busy place once again. Teachers felt free to write big posters, protesting their previous treatment.

A Rightist teacher wrote, "I resent having been labeled as a Rightist since 1957, just because I happened to tell an old story in class. The story went like this: An Emperor's first son was born, and he summoned his ministers to celebrate. The Emperor asked each of them to predict the baby's future. One minister flattered him, saying, 'This son is born an emperor.' The pleased Emperor immediately promoted this minister to a high position. The second minister observed the baby for a while and stated honestly, 'Please see a doctor, this baby is dying.' The Emperor was so enraged he had the minister executed. When the third minister's turn came, he didn't know what to do. He didn't want to flatter the Emperor with lies, but he was also afraid of speaking the truth. So he just muttered 'Oh, ya, ya, ya, oh, oh . . . ' This is a simple, traditional tale, yet I was accused of insinuating that Chairman Mao is like this emperor!"

Our trigonometry teacher wrote: "I was accused of living a decadent bourgeois life because I married Teacher Yu, who had deserted her fiance. Is there a law against a women deserting a fiance and marrying another man? They transferred my wife to a distant school, so that, as they put it, bourgeois decadence wouldn't influence my students."

Teacher Han, the teacher of foreign languages, wrote, "They put me in jail because I wrote 'Long live Chairman Mao' in characters that looked like 'No life Chairman Mao.' It was an accident because the character for 'long' is similar to the one for 'no.' Yet they accused me of condemning Chairman Mao to death."

Our physical education teacher wrote, "I was accused of being a Guomindang (Nationalist) spy because I had been a captain in a Guomindang unit. But I had already defected to the Communist Eighth Route Army in 1945."

The music teacher was the most vociferous. She told everyone that she had been accused of living a capitalist lifestyle because she had sung a love song in public.

"Why did you sing it in public?" I asked her.

"I sang it at my wedding party. I sang to please my husband," she answered.

But Teacher Tong, a Communist Party member who had been teaching political science, privately told me, "There's something wrong here. The situation has become so complex that you must remember to keep a cool head at all times. Observe and think carefully, and don't join the rightist teachers. They are trying to take advantage of the Cultural Revolution to shake off their political backgrounds."

"What do you mean by 'shaking off their political backgrounds'?" I asked.

"They are disgraced rightists. They try to use the Cultural Revolution to get rid of their rightist label."

Students began to be idle on the campus. They had nothing to do and were not interested in reading posters by the teachers. Finally, students stopped coming to school altogether. This was even true of the Woman Hero, who had gone to visit her relatives out of town.

I hadn't seen Suansuan for over a month. I went to the Small Town Inn many times hoping to meet her, but I never did. I, too, stopped going to the school campus. But I felt ashamed staying at home. I was nearly eighteen, yet still being fed by my father and stepmother. To have my parents see me sitting idle at home every day made me unhappy. As soon as supper was over each evening, I would go out to listen to the free lectures in the streets.

Actually, these free lectures didn't interest me much because the university Red Guards only shouted violent slogans. But I didn't like the mayor either. I couldn't understand why each time people ordered him to confess he would take them to a restaurant to eat.

Every evening I saw groups of idle students in the streets. One evening I met Fang, a classmate. He said he needed to find a job badly because he lived with his grandmother who was very ill. I asked him where his parents were. He told me that his mother was a rightist who had been sent away for labor reformation and his father had died.

"But we are not allowed to work because we are high school students, and must join in the Cultural Revolution," he said as he turned and went away.

I wish I could get a job, too, I thought. Life was dull and I was depending on my parents.

I thought of writing to Deng He. I longed for a friend I could talk to. But I didn't know where I could reach him. I had heard that all the Educational Work Teams in the countryside had by now been dismissed. Deng He must have returned to his university in Chongqing. But I didn't know the address.

In November, 1966, it turned very cold. I felt colder than ever before because I was very unhappy. Then, one day, to everybody's great surprise, an exciting policy was announced in the government newspapers: "All students and teachers in universities, high schools, and middle schools are now free to travel throughout China. This is called the Revolutionary Tour, and through the tour you are to share the revolutionary experience and gain understanding of Chairman Mao's great strategy for the Cultural Revolution. During the Revolutionary Tour students are to have free board and lodging anywhere. Every place must welcome them and take good care of them because they are Chairman Mao's honored guests."

Xiao Wu, a schoolmate and a Red Guard, came to invite me to travel with her. She had been born into a worker's family, and both her parents were restaurant cooks. She told me her sister lived in Qingdao, a beautiful coastal city in northern China. We could take a trip there and have a look.

We decided on the itinerary for our pilgrimage: Chong-qing, Guilin, Shanghai, Qingdao, Beijing, Chengdu, Zigong. The next morning we set out.

CHAPTER 6

A Revolutionary Tour

Students, rushing in every direction, thronged the train station. Nobody was in line. We couldn't even find a way to enter.

So we waited outside the station until late at night. When many of the students began dozing on the ground, Xiao Wu took me by the hand and we pushed our way to the entrance, where we climbed over a small iron fence before anyone noticed and dashed to the platform.

A train arrived, but all the doors remained shut. No passengers got off. When Xiao Wu saw some windows open, she boosted me onto her shoulders, urging me to crawl through. Struggling clumsily, I at last got my head to a ledge, where people inside took my hands, pulled me up, and helped me in. Xiao Wu was tall, strong, and capable. She raised her arms, took hold of the window ledge and quickly scrambled up by herself.

57

The train was so crowded that we stood pressed together, face to face.

"Are you O.K.?" Xiao Wu asked.

"It's kind of fun," I answered, and began to look around. Some people sat on the floor, some lay under the seats, and some were hunched in the overhead luggage racks, heads touching the ceiling, legs hanging down. As the train started, their legs swung with its movement. Some young men and women were hurtling over the seats, fighting their way to the bathroom. A loudspeaker on the train blared Chairman Mao's quotations one after another.

" You are youthful, like the morning sun at eight o'clock. You are the hope of China and the hope of the world."

" The Cultural Revolution won't occur just once in China, but many times. It will occur every year."

"Our proletarian government is a big tree and all the reactionaries are but little ants climbing upon it. When the wind blows, the ants will drop off."

"The reactionaries are but little flies, they hum about but will achieve only their death by hitting proletarian fists."

Standing there, listening to the litany of quotations I began to feel sleepy. To keep awake, I asked Xiao Wu why she had chosen me to tour with her since I was not a Red Guard. She said she had admired my singing and performances at school.

"That's nothing," I changed the subject. "Xiao Wu, have you ever seen my father? He is quite tall. And my own mother was tall too, but I am short. I don't know why. I hate being short!"

"I hate being big and tall," Xiao Wu laughed. "You know, in class, I was often afraid the teacher would see me first and ask me questions."

"I like to answer questions in class."

"Of course. You were always a good student, and all the teachers liked you. The math teacher often showed your homework to us, saying your notebooks were the most tidy. The English teacher kept a colored picture from a magazine under his table glass because the picture looked like you. Do you know how the music teacher interpreted your name in my class? Beautiful Sunshine."

"Please don't talk about the past. It doesn't count anymore. Now I'm not a Red Guard. You don't know how I feel wearing this silly Out-Circle arm band—that's what I am now, an 'outcircle.'"

"No problem," Xiao Wu exclaimed, "I can make you a Red Guard. You see, on your red arm band the three characters that form Red Guard are much bigger than the two characters below for Out-Circle. Let me fold the Out-Circle characters under, and people won't see them. Then you'll be a Red Guard, too." As she spoke she started fixing my arm band that way.

The train was so full that it moved slowly, and sometimes it stopped for hours with the doors closed. Though Xiao Wu and I ate only cookies and oranges, after twenty hours we both urgently needed to go to the bathroom. Fortunately, in the late evening the train finally stopped in the countryside, and all the doors were opened. It was a dark night. Every passenger had the chance to get off for a break.

The next day, in the late afternoon, the train entered Chongqing, Sichuan Province's largest city. It was dark and raining. Many people got off or, like us, were pushed off.

A large number of Red Guard Reception Desks had been set up at the station exit. We went to the nearest one— Chongqing No. 14 High School Reception Desk. After reading our student I.D. cards, two of the students took us into the school. They showed us the registration room where an old man received us and asked us how long we planned to stay. Two weeks, we answered. He gave us a handful of free food tickets, two quilts and two bed sheets, and told us to sleep upstairs.

Our room was a big classroom with twelve bed boards on the floor. After a huge dinner we went to sleep.

The next morning we went out into the streets, which were short, hilly, and with cable cars. We walked to the main street, the longest one, named Jiefang Bei Avenue, where countless little restaurants and shops were packed together. Their walls were plastered with posters, slogans, and cartoons. The first poster we saw announced: "The mayor of Chongqing is the biggest traitor of the City. He is a Guomindang agent." The illustration of the mayor was of a two-faced ghost. The next poster proclaimed, "The mayor is a murderer of the Chongqing people." In this one he was illustrated as an ugly man with a big, open, bloody mouth.

We went along with the crowds from poster to poster. At a theater gate, we came to a large oil painting of Chairman Mao and his wife saluting Red Guards. Beside them was an enormous red sun rising from a huge blue sea. The sun, I realized, was meant to be Chairman Mao, and the sea all the Chinese people.

At noontime, we went to a little restaurant and were pleased to find that they served delicious fish heads. We bought a big bag of them, and ate along the street. "Chongqing is famous for food," Xiao Wu said. "My parents often say that. My parents are both good cooks and they were both born in Chongqing."

"But our teacher told us that Chongqing is the leading

industrial city in Sichuan, so why haven't we seen any factories?" I asked.

She pointed to the other side of Jialingjiang River, "Look, there's some smoke. The factories must be over there."

Evening came, and parades began. The parade of old people was fascinating. They all looked around eighty, walking slowly. One old lady walked on the flank with a little paper flag in her right hand leading the shouting. She yelled haltingly "Down with," and the others finished, "the mayor." Then she shouted, "Defend," and the others finished with, "Chongqing city." Their voices were low, joining together in *basso profundo*.

Xiao Wu and I both enjoyed watching parades. They were exciting and invigorating to us. One evening we happened to see high school students parading, with the mayor in their midst, wearing a tall paper hat. The students shouted, "Kill the mayor! Throw him into the river and drown him! Beat the mayor to the ground, and stamp our feet on his back!" Xiao Wu rushed over to the mayor and shouted in Beijing dialect, "Down with the mayor!" The mayor quickly bent his head and his paper hat fell to the ground. He must have thought Xiao Wu was a Beijing Red Guard and been frightened, for Beijing Red Guards were most powerful at that time.

A week later, a roommate told us about a natural swimming pool in Beipei, 30 miles away. "The water is like a magician and can make your hair grow fast," she said. We went there the next day. Although we couldn't swim, we ducked our heads in. But when our hair dried, it felt like a helmet because of the chemicals in the water.

Near the pool was the Sichuan Foreign Languages Institute, which reminded us of Tong Yu, a former schoolmate who was studying there. We were lucky enough to find her standing right at the gate.

"Hi, we thought you might be away," Xiao Wu greeted her.

"No, I didn't go anywhere," was all Tong Yu said. She seemed to be in a bad mood.

"Why not?" Xiao Wu asked. "Now you don't need any money and can go wherever you want in China. You've never thought of visiting home?"

"No, I don't want to see anybody, especially people I know."

"Why?"

Tong Yu said nothing. It was obvious that she was unhappy, and I changed the subject. "Tong Yu, do you know anything about the Radar Military Academy?"

"Yes, it's a famous university in Chongqing. Every student there is intelligent and talented.

"Can it compare with famous universities like Beijing University and Qinghua University?" I asked.

"Yes, but the students in Beijing University or Qinghua University get no government support. In addition, the students must pay for their own tuition, food, and books."

"You mean the students in Radar Military Academy don't pay anything?"

"That's right. They don't pay anything. Instead, they are paid every month, and they get their uniforms, shirts, socks, schoolbags, wash towels, soap, even notebooks. And when they graduate they will earn the same pay as students from Beijing University."

"Are all the students in the Academy from the families of high-ranking officials?"

"Not necessarily. Some of them are from the families of intellectuals. But wherever they're from, they must be very talented students."

"Where is the Academy?" I asked.

"I really don't know. It's a secret because it's a military unit. The entrance has no sign. It is said that the address is in military code numbers."

On the campus we saw many old posters, but few people. Tong Yu explained that the other students had joined the Revolutionary Tour and had left the school a month before. At noon she invited us to her room to have lunch. As I entered I noticed a little photo on the corner of her desk. It was of a handsome young man, the son of one of our English teachers. He was a good fellow, I knew, but wasn't accepted at any university because his father was in jail. He found himself work pulling boats, a menial job. "She loves him," I thought, and I admired her. A university woman loving a boat-puller was something great enough to touch my soul. "She is an unconventional woman, a great and noble woman." I thought. Then I came to think of Deng He. "Is Deng He an unconventional and noble man? Does he have deep feelings for me?"

Chongqing was a very rainy mountain city. One afternoon, as we walked down a lane, it poured and we had to take shelter in a building. The gate was guarded by two armed military sentries. From the gate, I saw a little sign inside, on which there were many numbers. I asked the guards, "Is this the Radar Military Academy?"

"What do you want?" they demanded.

"I want to see my cousin," I lied. "He studies in that school."

"What's his name?"

"Deng He."

One of the guards went into the building. He came back and told me, "Sorry, he went to Beijing."

"Is this a university?" I asked.

"No. We're the army. Part of the university."

"What does the army do? Protect?"

"Kind of."

A university protected by an army? This amazed me. Suddenly, though, I felt sad for myself. Deng He, in a famous university, had money and military protection. I had no school, no job. I had nothing. Wandering in the street, I felt like a falling leaf. Where was my destiny?

Feeling sad, I decided to leave Chongqing. I asked Xiao Wu to return the remaining food tickets and we caught the night train to Guilin, our next stop. On the train I gradually felt better. Xiao Wu had been very happy, and told me the old man reimbursed her six yuan for the food tickets.

"How could that be, when we'd never paid for them in the first place?" I asked. She said she didn't know either.

Guilin was enchanting in the early morning sunshine. Through the yellow curtain of the train window I saw range after range of green mountains in the shape of dragons, tigers, horses, or elegant ladies. A sparkling river wound around the foot of the mountains. But we didn't get off at Guilin Station. People told us that once we got off at Guilin, so many students were already there waiting for a train to Shanghai that we would never be able to get on another one.

"We must go directly to Shanghai," Xiao Wu was determined. "It's one of the biggest cities in the world!"

We arrived in Shanghai the next morning. Shanghai station was well organized. People formed lines, and the station police brought us to a reception desk where we had morning tea and were assigned to stay in the Ministry of Foreign Affairs at Huang Pu River beach. A car took us there.

Our room was modern, heated, and furnished with sofas and a television set. Each floor had a bathroom with a flushing toilet and hot and cold running water. We took showers and then ran out to see the main street, Nanjing Road. The street was wide, clean, busy, and had a great many skyscrapers.

At Xiao Wu's suggestion, we first went to get a taste of Shanghai food. We chose beef soup, and found it delicious. Then we went to see the posters, tidily placed on walls along both sides of the streets. The first poster shocked us. It read, "Down with Liu Shaoqi!" He was the president of China. Xiao Wu grabbed my hand and we ran away. "It's better not to stand near a reactionary poster," she said, "people will suspect we wrote it."

The next day we heard there was a special double-decker train to Hangzhou, the most beautiful area in southern China. Since we were from Sichuan, we easily got tickets from an old Shanghai man. There was a tradition of Shanghai people loving those from Sichuan. The train was unusually clean and comfortable. We sat on soft seats. "This train must be made for high-ranking officials," I thought.

In Hangzhou we saw Xihu Lake, a lake named for a beautiful woman buried there who had died defending her motherland two thousand years ago. We also saw the Lei Feng Tower which is near the lake. A famous legend said this tower was built by a Daoist monk to crush a white snake who had changed into a lady, married a doctor, and helped him to make medicines to cure poor people. I hated the tower, I hated the Daoists, so I borrowed a pocket knife from a tourist to carve these words on a bamboo tree near it: "A thousand curses on the Lei Feng Tower! Long live the White Snake Lady!"

A rumor was spreading that the Revolutionary Tour would end soon. So, after hurrying through Hangzhou, we set off for Qingdao, the coastal city where Xiao Wu's sister lived. We found seats on the train and slept comfortably all night. The next morning we got off and hurried to visit Xiao Wu's sister. To my disappointment she was a chatter-box without really much to say. "My name is Gold Cricket," she announced, "an opera singer." Before we could even sit down she led us out to meet her street leaders and gave them all the gifts we had brought her. I didn't like that. I detested bribery. That afternoon I left them and went off on my own.

I went to see the Pu Hai Sea which surrounds Qingdao city. The sea was so large it seemed to stretch all the way to the sky. Along the shore I saw two young women search-ing for shells.

"Where are you from?" they asked, approaching me.

"Sichuan. And you?"

"Beijing."

"Beijing? How wonderful! Which school in Beijing?"

"The high school attached to Beijing University."

"Fabulous! Have you ever seen Chairman Mao?"

"Yes, three times," they told me. "The Old Man wears a red arm band from our school. He supports the rebel Red Guards."

"Rebel Red Guards?" I asked. The term was new to me. "What does 'rebel' mean?" They explained that there were two different types of Red Guards, the conservative Red Guards, formed by Red Sorts, and the rebel Red Guards, who would follow Chairman Mao to Jinggangshan Moun-tain to re-liberate China.

"In our school there is only one Red Guard organiza-tion," I said, half to myself, feeling uncomfortable. I thought of the Woman Hero.

"It must be a conservative Red Guard unit. Are you a

member?"

"I'm not a Red Guard yet." I told them. I took off my red arm band, and showed them the two characters hidden under the fold.

"What does Out-Circle mean?" they asked.

"It means a subordinate organization."

"Interesting. Never heard of that," one said.

"They said I was not qualified to be a Red Guard," I told them. They both laughed. One of them said, "Everyone is qualified. Anyone who wants to can become a Red Guard!"

"But . . ." I didn't know how to explain, so I stopped.

"Why don't you establish your own Red Guard, a rebel Red Guard organization like ours?"

"Can I really do that?" I certainly doubted it.

They laughed again and took a red arm band from their bag. "Put it on, and you will be a rebel Red Guard of our school. In Beijing, the students can join any Red Guard organization on their own. Our school has more than ten different Red Guard organizations, like every school in Beijing."

This surprised me. Before the Cultural Revolution, all organizations except the Communist Party and the Communist Youth League had been regarded as counter-revolutionary. I therefore asked, "What's the difference between all the rebel organizations and the Communist Party?"

"The Communist Party? You must be talking about another time. As you must know, the Communist Party was established way back in 1921. And now, most of the members have become capitalist roaders. We are Red Guards, established this year. To save China, we are fighting those old Communist Party members, and we will get rid of them. Chairman Mao has told us that half of China has turned to capitalism. The biggest capitalist is Liu Shaoqi."

"You mean Chairman Liu?" I couldn't believe my ears.

"Don't say Chairman Liu," one of the women said. "He's no longer the chairman. In Beijing we burnt all his photos at Tiananmen Square. We burnt Deng Xiaoping's photos too. The two are the biggest capitalist roaders in China. During the struggle meetings in Qinghua University we spat at Liu Shaoqi and hit him with the book of Chairman Mao's quotations. You know, Marshal Lin Biao will be the new chairman. Haven't you seen him standing beside Chairman Mao and Comrade Jiang Qing on Tiananmen Balcony saluting the rebel Red Guards?"

That night, lying alone in a big empty classroom at Shandong Ocean University, I couldn't sleep. I kept wondering how Chairman Liu could have developed into a big capitalist roader? What was a capitalist roader, anyway? What was a capitalist country like? I thought of the book written by Chairman Liu, *How to Be a Good Communist*, in which he called on all communists to devote themselves to the country and to care for people. He seemed a good man when I had read that book. How had he changed and become a capitalist roader? No matter how my thoughts wandered, I always returned to my belief in Chairman Mao, who led the Chinese people in defeating the Japanese invaders and the corrupt Guomindang regime. He is our greatest hero. He must want to do something good for China in launching the Cultural Revolution.

Then I turned to thinking about establishing my own Red Guards, and felt excited. For a long time, I had wanted to become a Red Guard and overpower the Woman Hero. "I will establish my own Red Guard, the Jinggangshan Mountain Red Guard Organization," I said to myself again and again.

As soon as I got up I went to Xiao Wu and urged her to return to Sichuan. I was eager to get started organizing as soon as possible. But Xiao Wu insisted on visiting Beijing before going home. "Beijing is the heart of the Cultural Revolution. We must at least take a picture of Tiananmen Square," she said.

Beijing was icy in December, and, as we got off the train at the Beijing station, the night winds cut into my face like knives. Standing in line to reach the reception desk, I suggested that we take turns, one of us in line while the other ran around the station. Otherwise we would freeze to death, I thought. Coming from Sichuan we had never imagined Beijing, or anywhere, could be so terribly cold.

The people at the registration desk arranged for us to stay in No. 8 High School behind Tiananmen Square, and we found space on the floor and went to sleep. In the morning I woke up and found seventeen other students sleeping on the floor around us, wrapped in quilts. Two nearby were talking:

"Why don't we change our Red Guard's name?"

"What name do you want to change to?"

"Revolutionary Torch."

"But I'd like Shaoshan Mountain, since Shaoshan is Chairman Mao's birth place."

As these two got up, I followed them to the washroom and asked, "Where are you from?"

"Nanjing," they replied.

"How is the revolutionary situation there?" I asked.

"The revolutionary situation is excellent." They both laughed at what they had said. It was the most popular political slogan. Then they asked me, "Where are you from?"

"Sichuan."

"How is the revolutionary situation there?" They were joking.

"Well," I said, "in my school there are only a few Red Guards."

"A few? Why?"

"I don't know. Most of them are from Red Sort families, only one or two are from the Gray Sort."

"Red Sort?" they laughed. "Lao Bao Red Guards."

"Lao Bao means conservative Red Guards?" I asked.

"Exactly. You don't want to belong to that capitalist organization, do you?"

Before I could say more, they urged me to establish my own organization. "This is the Cultural Revolution. Anybody has the right."

I woke up Xiao Wu and we went to Tiananmen Square to take pictures. Standing in the huge square, facing the magnificent People's Hall, the modern Museum of Chinese History, and the towering Monument to the People's Heroes, I felt tall and strong, and all my emptiness and sadness had suddenly disappeared. Beijing was beautiful, grand, and magnificent. Beijing—the heart of my motherland. I loved my motherland, my China. I felt proud to be Chinese. Looking around, I felt all thoughts of myself were gone. Why should I think of myself? Why should I worry about my own future? My motherland was most important. I should think about how to devote myself to my country, how to make it more and more beautiful, more and more magnificent. Living in this land, I should first serve this land. I went up to the massive photograph of Chairman Mao, hanging on the Tiananmen Square gate, and bowed to him, my heart filled with deep gratitude. "Chairman Mao," I pledged "It is you who have led our country to victory. I will be your most faithful Red Guard.

I will establish the Jinggangshan Red Guard Organization, and I will bring all my members to follow you to the Jinggangshan Mountains."

I drew Xiao Wu close to me and asked, "What do you think is the happiest thing in life?"

"I have no idea yet," she said.

"It's to do something important for our country!"

I led all the Jinggangshan Red Guards in a parade.

CHAPTER 7

The Jinggangshan Mountain Red Guard

井肖山兵团

In spite of four days on the train, I didn't feel tired. All the way home I was thinking about how to organize the Jinggangshan Mountain Red Guard.

At the dinner table I told my parents about what I had seen and heard on the tour. I happened to mention that Xiao Wu and I were reimbursed for returning the free food tickets in Chongqing. Father was indignant, "I can't believe you accepted that dishonest money. You must return it immediately." Mother joined in, "Even if there is a basket of gold left on the ground, you shouldn't look at it, because it doesn't belong to you." I shrugged. I didn't know how to explain it to them, and decided next time to keep my words to myself.

Next morning I hurried to school to make a big sign: "The Jinggangshan Mountain Red Guard is now established. We are enlisting those students willing to dedicate themselves to Chairman Mao, to his policies, aims, and revolutionary strategy. If necessary, we will follow Chairman Mao to return to the Jinggangshan Mountains to re-liberate China. Sign up, and you will become a member of the Jinggangshan Mountain Red Guard."

I nailed the poster to the school gate, and sat down by it to wait for candidates. Teachers came to read it, as did the school workers. And in the afternoon, students started gathering to read the poster and signed their names. By late afternoon, over a hundred students had signed up. I recorded their names in my notebook.

I remained at school till midnight, making red arm bands for my members. Before I went home, I left a note on the school gate announcing a meeting for the members the next morning.

We held the meeting in the library, the largest room in the school. I gave everyone a red arm band and said, "Now all of you are Chairman Mao's Red Guards, the rebel Red Guards. You are required to devote yourself totally to Chairman Mao, to listen to him, to read his books, and to do whatever he wants. Chairman Mao led our older generation to defeat the Japanese invaders and drive away the corrupt Guomindang regime. No Chairman Mao, no People's Republic of China. Chairman Mao is our great savior. Chairman Mao is doing everything good for our country. We have the good fortune to be able to join the Great Cultural Revolution and to defend Chairman Mao. We have the honor to be Chairman Mao's Red Guards." I continued, "Comrades, we must be faithful to Chairman Mao. We must follow Chairman Mao closely. We must let the revolution test our will. If some day the revolution needs us to go back to the Jinggangshan mountains to start a new uprising, we must go there. Believe in Chairman

Mao. Believe his revolution will win."

Everyone became excited and cheered: "Long live Chairman Mao! Long live the Cultural Revolution!"

I divided the members into four groups, and had each group elect three leaders. In the group leaders' meeting I asked them to train their group members according to the four military principles: to be alert, serious, united, and strong. I also taught the group leaders the military morning exercises that I had learned from Deng He and Yong Tian.

"You train your members every morning, I will inspect you," I said. "In the afternoon you lead your members in reading the newspapers and discussing the contents, because Chairman Mao's strategy and new policies are published in them."

That evening I led all the Jinggangshan Red Guards into the streets in a parade. We shouted: "Down with the capitalist roaders! Long live the Cultural Revolution! Long live our great, wise, and correct leader Chairman Mao!"

All the members were in high spirits. They raised their fists in the air and shouted. They were real Red Guards, ready to go wherever Chairman Mao pointed, I thought, and felt quite pleased with myself. I had organized a big group—like an army.

The members were mostly Gray Sorts, but gradually some Red Sorts joined in, and Black Sorts too. Seeing them wearing the Jinggangshan Mountain red arm bands, practicing military exercises, singing revolutionary songs, and talking enthusiastically with each other, I rejoiced. I wished Meimei were with me.

Remembering Chairman Mao's saying, "Political power grows out of the barrel of a gun," I invited several military men to come and teach us how to use guns, and I instructed the members to use bamboo poles for guns in practice shooting. I also led my guards in running with the bamboo poles up to the highest mountain near the school, so as to practice shooting down airplanes.

The Woman Hero now seemed idle, wandering about on campus or standing before a poster. She might come to ask to join the Jinggangshan Mountain Red Guards, I thought. But she didn't. Instead, two weeks later, she formed an organization of her own named "Shocking Thunder." She announced, "We are going to organize people to study the theories of Marxism and Leninism and the thoughts of Mao Zedong." She recruited three Red Sorts. The four of them carried thick books, *Das Kapital* by Marx, under their arms every day, pretending to be Marxist scholars.

I missed Suansuan. But I didn't know where I could find her. The area of her old home was under construction. I wrote to her at her parents' university, but received no reply. She must still be thinking I'm an opportunist, I thought.

In a few weeks my Jinggangshan Red Guards had grown to five hundred members, or ninety-five per cent of the students. To support us, our teachers established a similar organization called, "Jinggangshan Mountain Beacon." Teacher Wei was the leader. The teachers often joined our parades. When we marched in the streets, we sang old revolutionary songs from the years 1928 and 1929. This was the period during which Chairman Mao had led the famous peasant uprising in Jinggangshan Mountain. Our most popular song was:

Unite, all the people. Our hearts will twine together like a rope. The rope will whip to pieces the old world. Unite, all the people. Each of us is a brick. And all the bricks together will build a new world.

76

Unite, all the people. After the dark comes the dawn.
The sun is Mao Zedong.

Many students in other schools applied to join my Red
Guard unit, and many factory workers did too. One evening a group of more than four hundred workers joined our
parade and then asked to become members of our Red
Guards. They were from the Southwest Electronic Factory,
the biggest factory in our city. They shouted: "Long live
the Jinggangshan Mountain Red Guards! Firmly support
the Jinggangshan Mountain Red Guards!"

After the parade the leader of the workers told me he
was the new Communist Party Secretary of the factory. He
was around thirty years old. When I asked him where the
old Party Secretary was, he told me, "He was killed because
he shouted 'Long live chairman Liu' in the street."

I didn't believe that someone would shout such a
counterrevolutionary slogan in public, and I asked him,
"Has anybody else been killed?"

"Yes. Chang Pen's aunt, who shouted 'Down with Jiang
Qing!' She was caught on the spot by two policemen. They
cut out her tongue and slit her throat."

"Where did that happen?" I asked.

"In Liaoning Province. That is really true," he said
earnestly.

"How would you know it's true if it happened in another
province?" I didn't want to believe him, and went home.

On the way, a middle-aged man patted me on the shoulder. It was Mr. Lin, a lawyer of the District Supreme Court.
He invited me to give a lecture to his colleagues. I was
pleased, and immediately agreed.

The next afternoon I went to the Supreme Court, a
stately stone building surrounded by a high iron fence.

Lawyer Lin and about thirty of his staff stood at the entrance gate to receive me. In an office I sat down before them, and said, "I have been to Beijing and many other cities, and I have learned that the Cultural Revolution is a great revolution. Chairman Mao has launched it to rally all the people to fight and save China from the capitalist roaders. Did you know that half of China, although under the leadership of the Communist Party, has already changed color and gone down the capitalist road? The situation is dangerous, and Chairman Mao is determined, if necessary, to return to the Jinggangshan Mountains to start a new revolution to re-liberate China. I established the Jinggangshan Mountain Red Guards to enlist all the people who want to join in the Cultural Revolution, and to support Chairman Mao. I hope you will support us. You are powerful because you uphold the law. Your duty is to protect the revolution and the people."

I stopped. I didn't know what to say. I thought of Meimei. If Meimei had been protected by law, she would have still been alive. I said, "People need your protection, but are you true to your duty?"

I thought for a moment I might have offended them, but when I looked into their faces, they seemed very touched. So I continued, "There is a poor old man who was driven out to the countryside because his daughter-in-law accused him of being a capitalist. Isn't it terrible that an innocent old man should have been driven away by a family war? Where is the law?"

Then I remembered the bandit village where I worked for six weeks, and I said, "In one village I know of people who live a very poor life. Families don't even have enough rice bowls for meals. But ninety-five percent of the villagers have been classified as bandits for no reason at all. What's more, the village leader, a good man, had been accused of being a bad element because he spoke the truth. Comrades, what have you been doing to uphold the law?"

Everyone looked stunned. Perhaps they are feeling guilty, I thought, and quickly brought my speech to an end.

That evening, lawyer Lin invited me to have dinner with him in his home. While cooking, he asked me casually, "Can you define what a capitalist roader is?"

"A capitalist roader is someone who tries to change our country into a capitalist country," I said.

"Do you know what a capitalist country looks like?" he asked.

I couldn't answer his question directly, so I said, "According to our textbooks, a capitalist country is full of beggars who sleep in the streets. There are only a few rich people. They take their baths in milk, and they throw bread and rice into the sea instead of giving them to the poor."

"Have you ever listened to the Voice of America?"

"No, we are not allowed to," I replied. "Anyone listening to that station will be arrested. It is said the police station can trace the listeners by some special machine."

Lawyer Lin put the food he had been cooking on the table, saying there were a lot of problems in our country, especially in the Supreme Court. He then told me a true story: "Ten years ago, a fisherman came home one evening and found a dead body in his boat. He reported the case immediately to the local police, but as a result he was arrested. The local officials suspected that he was the murderer. Six months later he was put to death, leaving behind a wife and three little children. Seven years later the real murderer was found."

"Who decided to sentence that man to death?" I asked.

"Judge Chang."

"What was the punishment for Judge Chang since he killed an innocent person?"

"Nothing. He was transferred to another city and still remains a júdge."

"Still a judge?"

"Yes."

"So now he will kill innocent people in that city?"

"Yes, and then he will be transferred to another city. China has thousands of cities, enough for him to be transferred indefinitely." Lawyer Lin said this with anger.

"He must be a capitalist roader," I said. "He must have been protected by Liu Shaoqi, the biggest capitalist roader in China. China has so many problems. That's why our great leader Chairman Mao launched the Cultural Revolution, to deal with them."

Lawyer Lin said nothing.

Accompanying me home after the meal, Lawyer Lin asked me to visit him again. He told me that his daughter was the same age as I, a high school student. He also told me he had a great many detective books that he would be glad to lend me. "You are very intelligent," he said. "You may become a judge some day."

The Eight Revolutionary Operas revised by Comrade Jiang Qing, Chairman Mao's wife, were being performed in every theater in our city. We watched the operas, sang the operas and danced the operas. Anything from Chairman Mao and his wife must be correct, I believed. Chairman Mao was doing everything to save China.

The University Red Guards in our city had now established the Rebel Red Guard Headquarters, dedicated to leading the city revolutionary movement forward. Xiong, the Beijing Red Guard, my former schoolmate, was the Chairman of the Rebel Red Guard Headquarters. One day he called me to an emergency meeting with fifty other rebel Red Guard leaders at No. 1 High School. The purpose was to unify all of the rebel Red Guards in the city.

Xiong declared that the Revolutionary Headquarters consisted of three subgroups, the Command Ministry, the Politics Ministry, and the Fighting Ministry. He appointed me leader of the Fighting Ministry. "You will control the action of all the rebel Red Guards of the city. There are more than ten thousand now." Xiong introduced the other leaders to me, and I carefully wrote down their names, telephone numbers, and their schools or work units. I instructed them to report their work to me once a week, and urged them to train their Red Guards according to military principles. "You must discipline your members strictly, and I will inspect you at any time," I told them, believing that was my responsibility.

In late February, 1967, I received a package from Deng He. It was a green military uniform, and there was a note in it:

Dear Little Devil,

I am sending you this uniform, since many students in Beijing wear this kind of uniform, and Chairman Mao and Comrade Jiang Qing wear such uniforms when receiving the Red Guards on Tiananmen balcony.

I miss you every day, but I don't know how to find you. I went to your school once to invite you to travel with me to Beijing, but I was told you were away. Could you please send me your home address?

Deng He

"Chairman Mao himself signed it," Tan Wen exclaimed.

CHAPTER 8

Dark February

一月逆流

I wanted Deng He to visit me at my home, but I was concerned about my parents' reaction. They wouldn't like me to bring a young man home. My mother often said, "I don't believe a stranger, especially if he lives in another city." I told myself maybe I would see him after I got to know him better through his letters.

I was busy every day, attending all kinds of meetings at different schools. As the Fighting Minister, I was responsible for over ten thousand rebel Red Guards. Sometimes I had to visit factories in the countryside to check on the rebel Red Guards there, to inspect their activities and their training. Sometimes I went to other schools to listen to reports about their political activities.

One evening, I saw two police cars racing down the street with sirens screaming. Then three, four, five, at full siren blast. The next morning I heard a report on the local radio that I could hardly believe. It declared, "The government is going to arrest the counterrevolutionaries. All the rebel Red Guards are counterrevolutionaries, and all the rebel Red Guard Organizations are counterrevolutionary organizations."

All the government newspapers carried the same headlines: ARREST THE COUNTERREVOLUTIONARIES! The shock made me feel dizzy. I reread the newspapers and checked every word. There must be a mistake somewhere, I thought. How could the government newspapers make us counterrevolutionaries? It was impossible. We established the rebel Red Guards because Chairman Mao asked us. We led the rebel Red Guards in training, and in reading Chairman Mao's works because we were preparing ourselves to follow Chairman Mao to the Jinggangshan Mountains. Why did the government suddenly call us counterrevolutionaries and order our arrest? After breakfast, I went to school. I was sure something must be wrong with the reports from the radio and the newspapers. Chairman Mao would never allow anyone to arrest us.

On the school gate I saw a large poster, "To arrest Xiong Da Wei is a revolutionary demand!" Stunned, I asked the school gateman if Mr. Xiong had been arrested.

"Yes, last night. And your classmate Shen Min, too."

I felt terribly confused. Passing by the library, where I had held so many school meetings for the Jinggangshan Red Guards, I was sick to see another poster, "Down with the counterrevolutionary organization—Jinggangshan Mountain!"

I kicked the library door open. Inside it was crowded, with a meeting going on. Chairing the meeting was the Woman Hero. "To arrest the reactionaries is part of Chairman Mao's strategy of the Cultural Revolution," she was declaring. "The Cultural Revolution is a stage, where everyone shows off. Now that the reactionaries have shown off enough, we'll put them in the big black jailhouse. This is called 'to catch a big fish, cast a long line.' Thanks to the Cultural Revolutionary line that has helped us catch the fish, the reactionaries!"

I stood beside the door. Everyone was talking about Chairman Mao's strategy, but each speaker seemed to have a completely different idea about it. The strategy I knew was to train all the rebel Red Guards to follow Chairman Mao to the Jinggangshan Mountains. I looked at the Woman Hero, believing she wanted to use the revolution for her own evil purpose.

The meeting ended. As the people crowded out, Yulan, one of the Jinggangshan members and my close friend, indicated that she wanted to have a private talk. We walked off the campus. Yulan told me all the teachers had been sent back to the cowshed again, and a group leader, Shen Min, had been arrested. He had been taken from his bed by two policemen the night before. Other group leaders, such as Xiao Gao and Liu Peng, afraid of being arrested, had run away. "They will arrest you, I'm sure," Yulan told me.

"If they really want to arrest me, they should have done as they did to Shen Min last night," I replied.

"Listen to me, they will arrest you sooner or later. They arrested Shen Min early because he is from a Black Sort family."

"Do you really believe that? Shen Min might have done something that we don't know about. They will not arrest me, I know it, because I didn't do anything wrong, I didn't do anything against Chairman Mao's teachings."

"You are the highest leader of the Jinggangshan Mountain Red Guards," she said impatiently. "You are the Fighting

Minister. You must know, today's newspapers call all the rebel Red Guard organizations counterrevolutionary organizations. You must hide!"

"You mean I must hide right now? Where do you think I can hide?" I mocked.

"Go to my home! I live in Curve Lanes. There are no streets there, just narrow curving alleys. Police cars can't even get into any of them. You know, my house has three doors on three different sides, and at the back of my house are the mountains. If anything should happen, you could easily escape. My mother is a trusted person, living alone with me."

"Are you serious?" I asked.

"Yes. I am very worried about you."

"Have you considered that I might bring you trouble by hiding in your house?"

"Don't worry. Liao Yong will protect me. He is now working with the Woman Hero. They are like a pair of pants—working together so closely."

"How could such a person protect you?"

"Well, he's been trying to make me his girl friend. I will just pretend I am."

"But I will get your mother into trouble in her work unit."

"She has no work unit. She lives on my father's salary. My father is a road builder in Tibet."

I followed Yulan to the southern end of the city and entered her house. Her mother was short and limped; she dressed poorly, but she was a warm, kindly person. The first thing she said to me was: "What winds from heaven brought you here? I'm very happy to meet you. Yulan often says you are wonderful. When I see you, I believe you are wonderful." Saying this, she went into the kitchen and cooked us egg noodle soup.

After the meal, Yulan showed me the house, which had two rooms on the first floor, and one for me on the second. Yulan asked me to change into her clothes so I would not be easily recognized.

"Have you told your mother I am hiding here?" I asked.

"No. She doesn't care anyway. She doesn't know anything about politics. She can't read."

"I think we should tell her."

"No need. Listen, wear my clothes, cut your hair in my style, don't go out in the daytime, and I'm sure nothing will happen."

"Did you tell her my name?"

"Yes, but I changed your family name. I asked her to call you Xiao Li."

Before Yulan went back to school, I asked her to take a note to my house. I wrote to my parents, "I am fine. Don't worry about me."

I spent all afternoon alone in the room upstairs, with the window closed. Yulan's mother went out shopping because she wanted to cook us a good dinner. Confined like that, I felt very dull, and anxiously waited for Yulan's return.

When it was dark, Yulan came home. She looked upset, and told me my parents had disowned me. "Your father put up a poster at school declaring you are no longer part of the family." I looked at her for a long while, finding no words to say. I was sorry for my parents.

Yulan continued, "The police went to your home to arrest you. They tried to force your parents to turn you over. That's why your father put up that poster."

"What?" I was shocked. "How could it be?"

Yulan didn't give a direct answer, but reported more bad news, that Teacher Wei, the math teacher, and Teacher

Yang, the rightist teacher, had been arrested. She said countless police cars were driving through the streets. Many young workers and intellectuals had also been arrested.

My mind was in complete confusion. They had actually tried to arrest me. But why? I was a good person, I had been trying to do everything I could to follow Chairman Mao. I was a good student. I did nothing wrong. I was his most loyal Red Guard! Why?

Looking out, I saw it was dark. In the darkness after awhile, I saw a little star. Suddenly, I recalled a revolutionary song:

> Chairman Mao, you are the Big Dipper.
> Giving light in the dark,
> A lamp, guiding the way
> For walkers groping in the night.

The song made me feel better. "Yulan," I said, "Maybe Chairman Mao doesn't know our situation. How could he see his Red Guards suffering without trying to help? Chairman Mao will help us. We are his faithful guards and we defend his revolution. He supported us before and he will support us now, I'm sure." Saying that I felt happy again.

Yulan's mother treated me like an honored guest. She cooked fish, roast duck, and beef soup for me. She often remarked to me, "Your stomach is holding ink, because you speak like a big scholar." She never suspected I was in hiding, and she never asked me why I did not go to school. I didn't know what Yulan had told her about my plight. She loved Yulan, her only child, and she trusted her completely.

Yulan brought me newspapers every day, and slowly a week passed. One evening when she came home, she reported, "Mr. Xiong was badly beaten in jail."

How did you get that information?" I asked.

"Tan Wen told me. He is one of the university Red Guards. He got the information from a sentry at the jail."

"Where did you see Tan Wen?"

"In his house."

"What makes you visit him?"

Yulan smiled and then told me, "I met him on the street, and he invited me to his house. We knew each other from before. He used to be my neighbor. He is bright, studying at Chengdu Industrial University."

"What else did he tell you?"

"He obtained a secret document from his schoolmate in Chengdu. It says that to arrest the rebel Red Guards is to suppress the Cultural Revolution. The arrests were stirred up by a handful of capitalist roaders in the central government."

"Chairman Mao is going to save us. Right?" I jumped up with great joy. "Yulan, take me to Tan Wen. I must see that document!"

The next evening Yulan didn't take me to Tan Wen's house but up into the mountains behind her house. There, in a cave, waited Tan Wen, a tall, strong-looking man with an enormous beard. He looked like a foreigner, I thought.

The cave was deep and narrow. Yulan told me that all the caves on the mountainside had been carved out by Tibetans centuries ago. Following the light of Tan Wen's candle, we came to a turn where there were escape routes going in two directions, one north and one south. We sat down on the cool, damp, rocky ground. The wind whistled shrilly as it blew across the mouth of the cave.

Tan Wen opened a batch of pink papers, telling me, "Here's the Anhui Document issued by Chairman Mao. It states that the Anhui police have made a serious mistake by harassing and jailing rebel Red Guards there."

Under the candlelight I quickly read the document, which consisted of only a few sentences. A pink paper, signed "I approve" and "Mao Zedong."

"Chairman Mao signed it," Tan Wen said, with a gentle, hopeful smile. Yulan and I smiled too. Chairman Mao supported us, and he was going to save us and save the revolution.

Tan Wen seemed very excited, and said, "Let me teach you a new revolutionary song."

> Wild goose coursing the sky,
> Find your way to Beijing.
> Tell Chairman Mao all the rebel Red Guards love him.

The melody was beautiful. Tan Wen had an appealing voice, deep and warm. We sang it together softly, and I felt as if we were part of a mythological story. It was perfect to be sitting together with such brave, loyal comrades. I felt purified, as in some special religious ceremony. Each one of us was completely dedicated, I thought. The candlelight shone on Tan Wen's face, his expressive deep eyes and his hopeful smile. This made me feel that Tan Wen was a great hero.

Before parting, Tan Wen suggested that I make a declaration on the main street to popularize the Anhui Document. "Many people will listen to you since you are a leader." He told me he would get the document copied for distribution.

"I will," I promised. "When do you think is a good time?"

"Tomorrow evening," he decided. "I will organize people to protect you."

With Yulan, I made my way down the mountain.

"He is very handsome, isn't he?" Yulan said. "I like him."

"Does he like you?" I asked.

"Yes. We grew up together. You know, when we were children we played all the time. He taught me how to climb trees and find birds' eggs."

"I hope you two will marry," I said.

Yulan was very happy, for she patted my back, and said: "You are naughty."

Next evening Yulan accompanied me to the main street, where I recognized a group of rebel Red Guards with Tan Wen among them. None wore a red arm band. I walked up to the top of the stone steps of a movie theater in the center of the city, where people were standing around chatting, drinking juice or buying tickets. "Comrades," I began, "Our great leader Chairman Mao has signed a most important document—the Anhui Document, stating that to arrest the rebel Red Guards is to suppress the great Cultural Revolution. The arrests are a serious mistake. They must be corrected. Read the documents."

I spread the document copies on the street and people grabbed them up eagerly. I continued: "Be clear about this. Be faithful to Chairman Mao's policy. The great Cultural Revolution will succeed! The setback is temporary. After midnight there will be morning sunshine." The audience grew larger and larger and more enthusiastic. Just then a familiar voice called out:

"Don't talk like that! Come home!" It was my father. I panicked and ran down the steps and through the audience with Yulan close behind. My father ran after me. Tan Wen and the rebel Red Guards blocked my father's way.

Suddenly I heard a cry of pain from my father. He had been tripped. But I did not stop running.

CHAPTER 9

Fighting

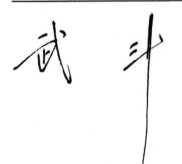

There were hundreds of caves in the mountains behind Yulan's house, and every night we met with Tan Wen in a different one to avoid detection. Tan Wen told us that many of his schoolmates had gone to Beijing to report the outrageous situation in Sichuan—especially how the Sichuan Rebel Red Guards had been arrested. Comrade Jiang Qing had seemed very concerned, and promised to report it to Chairman Mao, her husband.

A week later, Tan Wen came to Yulan's house to tell us Chairman Mao was going to help the Sichuan Rebel Red Guards by issuing a Sichuan Document. It would demand the immediate release of all the jailed rebel Red Guards. Tan Wen suggested I write an appeal to the Jinggangshan Red Guards, encouraging them to endure this temporary setback, this Dark February. The revolutionary dawn was near.

I wrote the appeal that very evening, and the three of us worked all night to make thousands of copies. The next night, after dark, we posted copies on every street corner.

At the end of March, 1967, the government issued the Sichuan Document on red paper. It said: "To arrest Sichuan rebel Red Guards is disrupting Chairman Mao's revolutionary strategy. All rebel Red Guards must be released immediately."

Airplanes dropped the red bulletins over the cities. I grabbed a bunch and ran the two miles to my parents' home to show them to my father. For the first time in my life, he hugged me, and apologized: "I should have supported you. Tell me what you need me to do for your Jinggangshan Mountain organization. I will do my best to assist you." My mother smiled. She had bought me a new jacket. However, she didn't say a word about the revolution.

I went to school to see my teachers, who were busy writing posters expressing their gratitude to Chairman Mao for releasing them again from the cowsheds and jails. They wrote: "Thank you, dear Chairman Mao, our savior. Thank you for releasing us from the cowsheds and jails. We will follow you closely, and carry out the Cultural Revolution to the end."

On the campus I saw Shen Min, my classmate. He had been jailed for three weeks during Dark February. I was very happy to see him, and I asked how things were going. "Bad," he spat out. "In jail they beat us with clubs." He tore open his shirt and I saw the welts on his chest. "They beat me front and back. They forced me to bake bricks naked."

"Bake bricks?"

"Yes, to bake bricks in gangs. Everyone naked."

"Why naked?"

"So it hurts more."

"How you must have suffered! But I don't think it will happen again. It is past. Let's forget the past."

"I won't forget! I will have revenge! I will kill all of them!"

The next morning I held a large meeting calling on all the Jinggangshan Mountain Red Guards to follow Chairman Mao's strategy, and to carry the revolution through to the end. I called on them to unite and bring more people into the revolution, to make friends with other students who were not yet Jinggangshan Mountain members, and even with those who had worked against us in the dark February.

We soon restored our training program according to military principles, and I checked the groups every day. The Jinggangshan Red Guard organization grew stronger than ever, with countless new students joining each day. I felt very good.

Deng He wrote me a letter. He was a Rebel Red Guard in his university, and he worked at the Chongqing Radio Station as the voice of the Chongqing Rebel Red Guards. "I am eager to see you," he wrote. "I hope we can sit together to talk about our exciting experiences in the revolution. I even hope that some day we will go together to the Jinggangshan Mountains. I feel I have so much to tell you."

I wanted to see Deng He very much, although I thought he was still a bit mysterious. I respected him, and I admired him. He was intelligent, talented, energetic, and handsome. He was too good to me, I thought. But I decided to invite him to visit me at my home the next week between three and four-thirty in the afternoon, when my parents would both be at work in their offices. I didn't want my parents to meet him yet. I felt too shy to do that, and the most important thing was that I was not sure he really cared for me.

On Thursday afternoon at exactly three o'clock, Deng He

appeared at my door. He wore a white sweater and blue pants, and carried a schoolbag on his shoulder. He was quite handsome. He blushed as he saw me. I must have blushed, too, because my face felt hot.

Sitting in the living room, we drank tea. We didn't speak much. It was difficult to find the right words. The clock on the wall chimed much louder than ever before. After some time, he gave me his bag, saying, "I nearly forgot that I've brought you some books, my old textbooks.

"University books?"

"Yes, I think you might like to read them since you will go to university soon. When the Cultural Revolution ends, all the universities will reopen."

"How long do you think the Cultural Revolution will last?"

"A few months, I guess."

"What university do you think I should apply for?"

"My university."

"To study radar?"

"Yes."

"But I'm no good at math."

"I will help you."

It was now about five o'clock. I felt nervous because my parents would be coming home in a few minutes. "Umm, would you like to go to a movie with me right now?" I finally asked. He stood up, and I hurriedly led the way out.

For two hours in the theater we watched a boring scientific program about cancer research. After the movie I thought he would say goodbye to me right away, but he didn't. I looked at him, but he looked back with no intention of saying goodbye. I was hungry, but didn't think I should take him to a restaurant because I was afraid my parents might be in one. It was no good to stand at the exit of the theater for a long while. At last I thought of a peach grove behind the theater, the only place I knew we could sit to have a private talk.

We sat under a peach tree, and he pointed to the full moon and asked me: "Do you like to watch the moon through tree branches?" I nodded and looked at the moon. It was strange to sit alone with a man. I was nervous, a bit excited, and a bit afraid.

The moonlight shone through the peach leaves down to the ground around us. It was lovely. Deng He looked at the moon, and then at me. And I did the same, looking at the moon and then at him. When our eyes met we both smiled.

He took up my hands and gently touched them. "Your fingers are delicate and beautiful. Many Tang poems describe the fingers of a beautiful young woman's as 'white heads of green onions.'" We both smiled again. "Your hands are so small, you see, I can use my one hand to hold both of yours."

"So hold them then," I encouraged him.

"No, that might hurt you," he said. "I will not hurt you." He held my hands and sang to the moon:

> The moon is over my head,
> The light is silver bright;
> Many nights I see the moon alone,
> Tonight . . .

Suddenly there was a noise, and a group of young men, dressed in factory clothes, came and shined their flashlights on our faces. "What are you doing here? Show your identities!" they shouted. Deng He stood up and gave them his military I.D. card. I was upset. Instead of telling them my real name I gave them my mother's. "I forgot to bring my I.D. card with me. Sorry," I said.

"You must leave immediately. If we find you here again we will turn you over to the police. This is the revolution!" they shouted and went away.

Next morning, I went to school as usual instead of going to Deng He's hotel to say goodbye, because I was still upset about the evening before.

On the campus, I saw Shen Min quarreling hotly with the Woman Hero, and many Jinggangshan Mountain Red Guards were watching intently. Yulan was there, too. "What's the matter?" I asked.

"He slapped me," the Woman Hero said, pointing to Shen Min. "Chairman Mao says there should only be verbal fighting, no physical fighting."

"She deserved it. I should have whipped her," Shen Min retorted angrily, and shook his fist in her face.

"Stop, Shen Min," I ordered, and grabbed him by his arms. The Woman Hero ran away. Shen Min threw me off, and shouted, "You protect her. You are terrible. You're not a revolutionary leader, you're a rightist!"

That afternoon Shen Min put up a big poster in the school dining hall. It announced that he had quit the Jinggangshan Mountain organization and had established his own Red Guard group—the "Dare to Die." On the signature lines at the bottom of the poster, hundreds of Jinggangshan guards had written their names, including Yulan. She told me I put too much emphasis on the idea of unity, when the revolution needs violence.

I reorganized the remaining members of the Jinggangshan Red Guards, and trained them to read the newspapers and to do the military exercises. But in the evening, when alone, I felt empty. My Jinggangshan Mountain Red Guard organization had split and Yulan, one of my best friends, who had hidden me in her own home for three weeks, was gone.

The local newspapers stopped mentioning the goal of going to the Jinggangshan Mountains. Instead, they encouraged the rebel Red Guards to fight physically against the conservative Red Guards. Comrade Jiang Qing made public speeches in Beijing praising physical fights. She called the fights "Attack with Words, Defend with Force."

The streets were now filled with noisy quarrels. Two or three Red Guard groups from different factions used Chairman Mao's quotations to provoke and fight each other. The arguments broke into street brawls. Factory workers, peasants, clerks, vendors, and soldiers all joined in the fighting.

"Peasants are a problem in China. They are selfish and conservative," one group would claim. An opposing group would retaliate, using another of Mao's quotations, "The peasants are a revolutionary force. They are brave, firm, honest, and the leading class in China."

"Chairman Mao says eating is of first importance in China. Without peasants all of you would starve to death," a peasant would add.

"But Chairman Mao says, 'Class struggle is the most important. No class struggle, no new China,'" a factory worker would lash out. "We would rather eat communist weeds than capitalist grain."

I often listened to them, trying to figure out who was right and who was wrong. In the end, I always decided that both sides must be right because both quoted exactly what Chairman Mao had said.

Xiong, the Beijing Red Guard, was released in May. He was the last rebel Red Guard to be released. That day over a thousand people gathered at the gate to greet him. As soon as he came out, two strong men lifted him on their shoulders, shouting with joy, "Our Xiong comes home!" Then the crowd started a big parade down the street. I joined in.

One evening at dinner time, two street leaders came to my home and asked my parents to donate money for erecting statues of Chairman Mao at the train station. My mother gave one yuan, my father, two. A few days later the street leaders came to ask for donations again for another statue in the city playground. Everybody had to contribute; it was a revolutionary requirement. When the statues were being constructed the streets were clogged and cluttered with materials.

Shops now started selling a great many kinds of Chairman Mao pins. They were made of metal, porcelain, or bamboo, and showed Chairman Mao with a raised hand, or standing on a ship. Everyone had to buy a pin to wear. This became another revolutionary requirement. The pins were inexpensive and I bought many. Some of them were beautiful, indeed. My parents sometimes received free Mao pins from their work units, and one night my father brought home a red one, big as a dinner plate.

The neighborhood committee leaders often asked my parents about street meetings they were to attend in the evenings, and ordered them to put Chairman Mao's picture on the wall of our home. "Every morning you must ask Chairman Mao, The Old Man, to instruct you, and every evening you must report to him," they lectured. "Besides this, you must dance the Loyalty Dance whenever we ask you to."

My mother was very unhappy because she had never danced before. However, the Loyalty Dance was taught everywhere in the streets, so I learned it and taught it to my parents. It was not difficult—just stretching your hands toward the sky and then drawing them back to your stomach to symbolize the idea that Chairman Mao was the sun rising from the heart to the sky.

The meaning of the Loyalty Dance, as the instructors explained, was: "Oh, our beloved Chairman Mao, you are the golden sun rising from our hearts. The natural sun rises in the morning and sets in the evening, but you, the golden sun, will never set. You shine on us day and night and brighten our hearts. Oh, beloved Chairman Mao, even though there are more than ten thousand words, they are not enough to express our thanks to you. Even though there are more than ten thousand songs, they are not enough for us to sing our thanks to you. We give you our loyal hearts and wish you a ten-thousand-year-long life."

In July 1967, I went to visit lawyer Lin. I asked him why Chairman Mao's sayings were contradictory and made people quarrel. His reply was, "Chairman Mao's sayings are not the Bible."

"Bible?"

"Yes," he said. "The Bible is supposed to be a book of truth that does not contain contradictory statements."

"I would like to read that."

"It's not available anymore. All such books have been burned. But perhaps after the Cultural Revolution it will be reprinted again."

"When do you think the Cultural Revolution will end?"

"Nobody knows, probably not even Chairman Mao himself."

"Why?"

"The revolution has gone out of control."

After we had dinner I said goodbye and started home. The streets were crowded with people reading posters along the street walls, or exchanging Chairman Mao pins, or quarreling over Mao's quotations.

So many people had gathered in the streets that the noise was tumultuous. The stench of sweat was strong, and so I decided to turn into a little lane that led to my home. Just as I reached the lane, I heard a deafening explosion and was knocked down by someone thrown on my back by the force of the blast. He was groaning with pain and holding his left foot, which was bleeding. His heel was gone.

I didn't know what had happened, but I heard the cries of many people who were lying in pools of blood on the street. Then ambulances screamed up to take the injured away. After the young man I was supporting was taken to the hospital, I walked slowly home, my teeth chattering. I was too scared to utter a word to my parents.

That night as I undressed for bed, I found a burn hole in my pants, as big as my finger. The next morning we were told that a student had thrown a grenade into the street during a quarrel with another young man over Chairman Mao's quotations. They were both killed. Six other innocent bystanders were killed with them, and forty-seven people were badly injured.

An anger started to burn inside me. I began to question why Chairman Mao's quotations made people criminals and caused so many deaths. These new doubts made me miserable. The Cultural Revolution now depressed me. Every evening I took a long walk alone.

On a rainy night, during one of my long walks, I saw a man through the dim light standing at the edge of the river. He stood still there for a long while, which made me curious, and I walked down to him. Near his feet I noticed something shining—a watch—and a wallet. I realized he was going to jump. Quickly I picked up a little rock and threw it into the water. He turned. It was Teacher Tong, my political instructor, a Communist. "What are you doing here, Teacher Tong?" I asked.

He was silent for a moment, then spoke, "I'm meaningless in this world." He coughed, and said he had been beaten in school. Students had blindfolded him, used stools to hit him, then locked him up for the night.

"Did the Dare to Die Red Guards beat you?" I asked.

"Yes, and the Shocking Thunder Red Guards, too.

"The Woman Hero?"

"Yes. She demanded I recite twenty of Chairman Mao's quotations. I wasn't able to recite every one of them, so she beat me and yelled that beating a capitalist roader is a revolutionary duty."

We walked silently along the river in the rain. At last I found words for him, from ancient Chinese philosophy: "Turn back one step and there is a way." These were words he himself had once taught me in class. I didn't know what else I could say to him.

Soon, battles were exploding everywhere in our city, and beating up capitalist roaders became a "fashionable" thing. According to the newspapers, to fight against the capitalist roaders was the most important aspect of Chairman Mao's revolutionary strategy for the Cultural Revolution. Many people would beat a so-called capitalist roader just for fun.

In No. 1 school, three rebel Red guards ordered their Party Secretary to sing a Quotation Song in public. He did. Then they ordered him to dance it. He didn't because he didn't know how, and for this he was badly beaten.

I grew more and more miserable because the Jinggang-shan Red Guards were all leaving to join Shen Min's group. They seemed eager to fight. I stayed at home all the time, feeling idle and wasted. I tried to read Deng He's textbooks but I couldn't understand the complex math formulas.

Every day I cooked for my parents or went to the markets.

One afternoon I heard some music near a market, and I went over to have a look. It was a dance group performing free entertainment. In the group was Linlin, one of my childhood friends, dancing ballet. We had studied together in middle school for three years. Her nickname in school was "The Fairy." She had long hair that shone like black silk and her cheeks were always pink, with two deep dimples. Her eyes, as my schoolmates said, "could be found only in a beautiful painting."

Linlin was dancing "The White-haired Girl," one of the eight model operas revised by Comrade Jiang Qing. After she finished, I went to talk to her and to ask how she had come to learn ballet.

"I learned it from Dai Hui. She is a professional ballet dancer."

"How did you become interested in ballet? It's very difficult, isn't it?" I asked.

"It's difficult, but I had to learn it!"

"Why?"

"This is the only way for me to join the Cultural Revolution.

"I don't understand."

"I'm from a Black Sort family. If I hadn't joined the Cultural Revolution, I might have been accused of class hatred against the Communists. But if I had joined some kind of rebel Red Guard organization I might have been arrested like so many during the Dark February. So I learned to dance ballet. It causes less political trouble."

"Linlin, will you come to my house?" I didn't want to talk politics in public.

In my house, she told me that her father had been a Guomindang official before the Communist Liberation. He

103

was arrested in 1951, and sentenced to death. He died in 1960 in jail.

"How old were you then?

"Three."

"You have a brother and sister, don't you? How does your mother support such a big family?"

"She knits sweaters for people."

"That is all? How much does she earn a month?"

"Twenty yuan."

"Oh, Linlin!" I exclaimed. When I was younger, I had never known Linlin lived in such difficulty. This made me feel guilty, as I remembered my ninth birthday. That morning Linlin brought me a cooked egg and a cookie, saying 'Happy Birthday!' Without a word of thanks I ate them up. Later, I learned from her mother that the birthday gift from Linlin was her school lunch meal. I was too young then to appreciate her friendship, which was so sincere she starved herself for a whole afternoon. Linlin. She was nine too, only half a year older than me.

I had to repay her. "Linlin, do me a favor," I asked her. Let's go to Mount Emei, to see the most beautiful temples in China."

"I don't have the money to pay the cost. Since the Revolutionary Tour has stopped, everyone has to buy train tickets."

"I will pay. My parents give me a monthly allowance, and I've saved enough for both of us."

"It's very kind of you. I've always wished to go there. But I'm afraid."

"Of what?"

"I don't know. I just feel afraid. You know, even during the Revolutionary Tour I didn't go anywhere."

"Linlin, come with me this time," I begged and held her hands.

I felt I was intruding on something sacred. . .

CHAPTER 10

Gold Top

上 金 頂

Linlin arrived the next morning with four boys and three girls. They carried violins, flutes and a Pi Ba, an ancient moon-shaped instrument. "My friends," Linlin announced happily, "they are organized into recreation cells, and they can dance, sing and play musical instruments. They're coming to the mountains with us. I invited them." I was glad to see them. They all looked energetic and had romantic manners. We exchanged greetings all around and boarded the bus.

We got off at the train station, and one of the boys offered to buy tickets for everyone. On the train he whispered to me that a ticket cost only thirty cents because he had bought tickets only to the first stop. "But how will we get by the ticket collector when we get off the train at Mount Emei Station?" I asked. "It's the fifteenth stop."

"Never mind. I can manage. I will get off to buy more

tickets when the train arrives at the last stop before Mount Emei station," he reassured me.

The train was in good order, not crowded at all; there were seats for all the passengers and the floor was clean. The train sped along and soon we arrived at the eighth stop, Xin Du Station. Just then a conductor came into our car to check tickets. He wore a tight blue uniform and carried an electric prod.

I became nervous, and the others in our group turned pale. I watched the conductor, trying to figure a way out. When I noticed he didn't check every passenger an idea came to me: distract him.

I got my group together to play music, and asked Linlin to dance. "Go to the center of the car so that everyone can see you," I said in a low voice. "Do your best."

The music was cheerful, Linlin danced beautifully, and all the passengers stood up to watch her. Even the conductor came over. He seemed to enjoy the program very much, and he smiled. I went up to him. "Excuse me, sir, I have a little problem I'd like to discuss with you." He nodded, and led me to his office in the next car.

"Sir, I am the leader of this recreation group, bringing them to perform the eight revolutionary operas in the area around Mount Emei. As you know, to perform the eight model operas is the current revolutionary task, since they were revised by Comrade Jiang Qing. But I'm sorry to tell you, we are only high school students so we don't have enough money to buy the full tickets." He didn't respond.

"Sir, do you think there is a possibility that we might buy the tickets now? I could ask the passengers to donate the money to us."

"These days many peasants don't buy tickets," he said. "They took advantage of the Revolutionary Tour when the policy allowed the students to have free trips.. Now the Tour is over. Everyone must buy tickets. If I catch one who fails to buy, I will fine him. If he refuses to pay, I will beat him with the electric prod." He stopped. I looked at him, wondering what would happen. Then he said, "But I trust you. You are a good person, I can tell. So this time I forgive you."

"But Sir, could you tell me how we'll get off the train when we arrive at Mount Emei station?" I asked very politely.

"I will help you," he replied with a kind smile.

The train moved along, and by five o'clock in the afternoon Mount Emei came into view, massive and green, filling up all the windows of the train. We couldn't see the top, which was hidden in clouds of thick purple mist.

Before the train stopped the conductor came and told us to follow him. He didn't take us to the exit, but to a side door on the left side of the platform. Past the door we found a little room, his night-duty shelter. After he treated us to some noodles, he sent us out on the road. As we departed, he promised to bring us home from this station and told us he would be on duty next week in the same train, in Car Six again.

We walked for half an hour and arrived at the foot of Mount Emei. At the gate to the first pavilion we saw a paper sign: "Reception Room for Red Guards." Beside the paper sign was a big poster written in ink: "I am the father of Mount Emei. If I like, I will use a bomb to explode it." The signature was "Your father." The poster had probably been made by some Red Sorts at the beginning of the Cultural Revolution, during the campaign to destroy the Four Olds, when such abusive posters were popular. As we read the poster, a monk leaned out the pavilion window and bowed to us. "Welcome," he said. He bowed so low that I saw the nine burnt points on the top of his head which every monk carries to signify the forgetting of all his relatives and life outside the temple.

The monk registered us in two rooms, one for boys, the other for girls. We left our bags and ran to the nearby river. A big dead tree was laying across the stream. We walked and danced back and forth on the tree and sang songs. We were so happy that we shouted: "Long live Mount Emei!" For a long time our voices echoed over and over through the valleys.

Our rooms were on the second floor of a small temple to the left of the pavilion. They smelled musty. Linlin called this a "monk smell."

The next morning we saw many groups of monks in black robes quietly sweeping the yard. We ate our breakfast downstairs where two young monks served us corn bread and pickled bamboo shoots. The monks kept silent. After breakfast we went to see the temples. The main one was called Bao Guo Shi, "Defend the Country Temple." It was connected to many smaller side temples. All the Buddha statues had been destroyed. They were in pieces piled here and there. A large green jade statue was lying on the ground with broken arms and legs. Examining the fragments, we saw that the statue's face had modern black eyeglasses painted on it.

None of us was happy to see these desecrated statues, so we decided to climb up the mountain to the Qin Yi Ge Pavilion. We arrived there about two o'clock in the afternoon. It was a little black temple surrounded by colorful wild-flower gardens. There were no statues in the temple, only an empty altar and a black wooden desk. We left.

About fifty feet away to the north, we saw a waterfall

hanging over a high hill. The waterfall spilled into a pond. At the center of the pond stood a narrow, tall rock carved with characters that said, "Holy Pond." Two monks were standing by the pond, carefully throwing coins into the water as if to predict the future.

About three o'clock, we started climbing up to the third temple, Elephant Temple. It was said that the temple was white, and had many elephant statues in it. The elephant symbolizes loyalty.

The mountain road was so rough and steep that sometimes we had to crawl on our hands and feet. The many monkeys that Mount Emei is famous for chattered around in the trees and imitated our crawling. They liked our cookies and enjoyed stretching out their hands begging for more.

We arrived at the Elephant Temple in the evening around ten o'clock, very tired. We registered for rooms and went to the dining room to eat. The meal was cold rice and pickled green pepper. In the midst of eating, Xiao Liu, the youngest in our group became sick, and vomited. I took her to the bedroom, and on the way she vomited again.

I sat by her bed and asked the others to rest. Around twelve o'clock she was sick again. To wash her, I carried a basin to the dining hall, the only place where water was available. There, at a table two scholarly-looking women were gently drinking tea. "Hi little girl. Why are you still awake at midnight?" one of them asked.

"A friend is sick. I came to get her water."

"What's the matter?" the other asked with concern.

"The food doesn't agree with her, I guess."

"Let me go see her, I have some medicine for stomach troubles." She excused herself from the other woman and followed me.

She examined Xiao Liu's tongue and hands, and then said, "Don't worry, she is just tired. Have her drink some water, and keep her warm. She'll be all right."

"Are you a doctor?" I asked.

"No, I'm a writer, studying at Jilin Teachers' University." Her voice was crisp and clear.

"A famous university. I've heard of it," I said with admiration.

She smiled, and invited me to go outside with her to watch the moon. "This temple is the place for monks to watch the moon," she explained.

"Do monks enjoy watching the moon?" I asked. "I never knew monks had such an interest."

"They do. They believe the moon is one of the places of heaven. They believe they will go there after they die. They put all their unfulfilled hopes in the afterlife."

"Do monks also believe they can defend the country after they die?" I joked, "since the first temple is named 'Defend the Country Temple.'"

She smiled. "Many people have tried all their lives to get a chance to defend the country, but the ruling class refuses to give them a chance. Never give them a chance, but kill them—that is Chinese history. That's why many men came to the temples to become monks. Some of them are very intelligent and talented."

"How do you like the moon tonight?" she asked.

"The moon seems much bigger here. It seems covered by a veil."

"How old are you?"

"Eighteen."

"A golden age. You will succeed."

"Succeed in what?""

She didn't answer, but asked another question. "What

are you going to do when you grow up?"

"I don't know. I want to study in a university."

"What do you want to study?"

"Anything but mathematics."

"Have you ever thought you would be a writer?"

"No, but Suansuan, my friend, wants to be a writer. She is talented."

"You will become a writer."

"Me? Why do you think so?"

You have the qualities of a writer. First, you love people."

The word "love" sounded too strong. To take care of a sick person like Xiao Liu was my duty, I thought. She continued. "You are sensitive, imaginative, and romantic."

"My father hates the word romantic," I said. "He believes that it is a bad word. Every time he hears me singing songs, he calls me a romantic fool."

"But it is a good word. It's a very important quality for a writer. Have you read *The Dream of the Red Chamber*?"

"Yes, it's one of my favorite novels. It protests the cruelty of feudalism in China."

"True, it is a criticism of feudal society, but it is also a romantic book. Have you read *Li Sao*?"

"Oh yes. A long, sad poem written by Qu Yuan, who died two thousand years ago."

"Qu Yuan was a romantic writer. He wrote that poem to try and persuade Emperor Chu to care for the people. He failed, and was exiled by the Emperor. In despair he jumped into the Milo River. But his suicide didn't change the Emperor at all." She paused. "This is Chinese history, one dynasty falls, another rises, but emperors remain the same, doing whatever they like, never concerned about the people. Under one emperor the whole land is enslaved and whipped."

She grew angry as she spoke. She must have been writing

about Chinese history, I thought, and asked, "What have you been writing?"

She told me she was writing a play.

"What is it about?"

"Our daily life. About how to be an honest citizen living in our land. It is difficult to be an honest citizen, since many people have been trained to lie." She looked at me with determination. "Everyone has tears, as the sun has light, as the tree has leaves; everyone has a voice, as the birds in the trees. But we are taught not to be free and see and talk. Even if we see a donkey, we must say it is a horse."

She went on, "As a writer, one must write honestly to be true to life, to the people, and the land."

Listening to her, my thoughts turned to the beginning of the Cultural Revolution, and I thought of Meimei.

"Are you thinking about something?" she asked gently.

"I am thinking about my friend Meimei. She is dead. She was discriminated against in the revolution. She committed suicide. I miss her."

The woman took my hands in hers. "Will you tell me why you came to Mount Emei, a place for monks?"

"I don't know. I had never thought about coming here, until one day I saw my friend Linlin, and she told me her father had died in jail. I invited her to this mountain to make her happy."

"Write your thoughts down," she said, looking into my eyes. "I like you very much. At the first sight of you, I felt I had known you long before. I even felt I saw my own childhood. You are exactly like me. Write. I believe you will write a beautiful book someday. It is an obligation to our generation living in this land. Write everything that is in your mind. Write honestly. Honesty is the greatest beauty in writing."

114

It was about one o'clock in the morning. She gave me her address and I gave her mine. We wrote under the moonlight. Her name was Tao Kuang, which means to search for gold in the sand. The next morning I would climb up to the top of the mountain, Gold Top Temple, and she would go down to the foot of the mountain. Standing at my door, she held my hands for a long time before saying good night.

At five o'clock I roused everybody. We hurriedly finished breakfast, took a look at the white stone elephants in the temple, and started climbing toward the Gold Top, the highest temple on Mount Emei, 3,800 feet above us. This was the highest Peak of Mount Emei. It would be a long journey, about fourteen hours.

When we reached the second hill we saw the Ninety-Nine Steps, a steep stone stairway curving up into the sky. The path became as narrow as my foot. At the fifth step, Linlin told me that she was unable to continue and would go back to the Elephant Temple. She felt her heart pounding. Xiao Liu asked to be left behind, too. She was still weak from her sickness. The other girls tried a few more steps, and retreated. I pressed on with the four boys.

At the top of the Ninety-Nine Steps, we came to the Seven Fairies. These were seven dark tunnels that connected to each other and went through to the other side of the mountain. Hand-in-hand we groped our way in the dark holes. As we emerged on the other side, we saw a wooden bridge suspended between two peaks, in front of us, overhead, about five feet wide. It was the Bridge of Heaven. We had to cross it before arriving at the Gold Top Temple. Suddenly, a downpour started and each of us got as wet as a chicken in water. We uprooted some weeds to bind around our shoes, to prevent slipping on the muddy bridge.

Half an hour later, we were over the bridge, and it became very sunny. We gathered some sticks from the ground to make a fire and dry our clothes and hair.

Around seven in the evening, after passing through two woods, we saw Gold Top, a large gold structure, well-preserved, standing solemnly in its aura and dominating the vast world. It was now snowing. At the foot of the mountain it had been summer, but here it was winter. The monks brought us thick quilts to wrap ourselves in.

Gazing at the temple as we stood in the snow, we saw hundreds of gold bells around the edges of the roof, each as small as a fist. On the top of the roof we saw a big ball, as large as a basketball. With the wind, all the bells sounded like thousands of birds singing in spring.

That night I heard music. I got up and went downstairs to the main chamber of the temple, which had been closed before nightfall. I quietly went in, and peeked through a crack in the door. Sixteen monks wearing yellow robes were sitting in two lines on hard pillows. With bowed heads, they recited scriptures while their fingers slowly traced the beads around their necks. Many statues of Buddha in different positions were arrayed behind them. Some smiled, but most had wide open, fiery eyes and red mouths. One monk in a red robe was standing, knocking a stick against a little block of wood on the desk in front of him. His knocking produced a rhythmic beat that accompanied his recitation. I felt it was too sacred a scene for me to witness, so I went back to bed.

Morning came. All the tourists went out, carrying quilts on their backs. Pine trees were covered with snow. The sun emerged: red, clean, without glare, as if it were washed from a sea below. I saw the Sacrifice Valley Rock now on a cliff at the left of the temple, a square rock, 18 inches wide, where every monk on this mountain must stand in his old age, praying for a good afterlife before jumping into the deep valleys—their heaven.

The sun was rising, just in front of me. It was so close I felt I could reach my arms to touch it; the clouds were floating from one tree to another, and sometimes around me. The roof of Gold Top was in thick, moving clouds, changing colors from gray to yellow, red, purple and blue.

CHAPTER 11

At Sichuan University

四川大學

Funeral ceremonies were being held everywhere in our city. They were for those who had been killed defending the city against an attack by conservative Red Guards from Chongqing City. Returning from Mount Emei, I did not feel at home. I felt like a stranger.

The funeral music was heavy and people marched behind the coffins, wearing black arm bands and white paper flowers. There was no longer any city government; the army was in charge. Posters on the walls were even more violent and abusive than before. Many were written in dirty language.

The students in every school were split into two opposing groups, conservative and rebel. In many factories, institutes, and families, people were also divided along these lines. Everywhere there were fights, quarrels and cursing.

From my window I saw all the streets were put under

martial law every night. Groups of young people in blue uniforms wearing a special red arm band with the characters, "Workers' Supervision Team," patrolled the streets. They carried rifles and called out passwords to each other now and then. At night, occasional gunshots could be heard. One afternoon a group of men in their fifties carried a dozen machine guns up to the roof of our apartment. All night the machine guns rattled away. I couldn't sleep and neither could my parents.

I decided to leave. I would go to Chengdu to see my great aunt, the sister of my own mother's mother. My father opposed my decision. Father was a very honest man and very loyal. He always believed that the leadership was correct and that everyone should therefore obey them. He scolded me, "The army calls on every citizen to defend our city. Why do you want to flee? You should prepare to contribute your last drop of blood to defend our city." I didn't listen to him and left home that afternoon, catching the night train to Chengdu. I arrived in the city at midnight. As I got off the train I heard many shots, as if hundreds of guns were being fired. We passengers were ordered to stay the night in the station. I followed others to a waiting hall, and sat on the damp, cement floor that was covered with coal dust.

The next morning I walked to my great aunt's home. "Well, from where comes such a black monkey?" great aunt greeted me at the door.

I grinned. I knew my face must have looked funny all covered with coal dust. I took a bath, had some breakfast, and then my aunt brought me a sky blue dress to wear. As I was putting it on before the mirror, she turned away, wiping tears from her eyes.

"Dear Aunt, have I done something to displease you?

Am I not a good girl?" I asked, knowing she was always sentimental.

She shook her head. "I was thinking of your mother. When you put on this blue dress, you look so much like her. She died young, you know, died for her friend."

"Father said she died of tuberculosis."

"That's true, but she got it because of her friend Bai Ping. When Bai Ping developed tuberculosis nobody would look after her, not even her husband. Everyone was afraid of getting the disease too. So your mother went to take care of her and caught TB. Your mother was such a kind woman. Everyone loved her. She was beautiful."

I changed the subject, and asked about the gunshots outside the station last night.

"It's the war between the 8.26 group and the East Is Red group, two student Red Guard groups in Chengdu," she explained.

"Students? And they use guns? How can students get so many guns?" I exclaimed with surprise.

"Chengdu has now split into two groups. The 8.26 organization represents Sichuan University, and the East Is Red represents Chengdu Communications University. All the high school students belong to one or the other of these two groups. It's the same with all the factory workers, clerks, even the doctors and nurses. The worst of it is that armed troops have joined both sides. They supply guns to them. You know, in Chengdu there are many war equipment factories whose workers joined these groups. They produce guns, shells, and cannons for them! They shoot at each other every night. They have been shooting for two months now."

"The two sides are the conservative Red Guards and the rebel Red guards?"

120

"Right."

"Have you joined the groups?" I asked.

"No. I'm seventy-one years old. I don't get involved in those things. You know, when they fight, they wear nothing but underwear. They climb to the roofs of buildings to shoot at each other."

"Why do they only wear underwear?"

"To save clothes for their families, because they might die any minute. Every night when it gets dark they start shooting."

"Why don't they shoot in the daytime?"

"I don't know. I guess they have to go shopping in the daylight. They have to buy things to eat."

"Aunt, do your two sons join in the fighting?"

"I don't want to talk about them. I hate both of them. They are both train workers, yet they don't even speak to each other anymore. They have taken different sides."

"Do they visit you?"

"They come to give me money once a month, that's all."

After lunch her grandson, Jia Yong, arrived, a tall, pleasant-looking young man from Sichuan University. "Hello, Brother Yong, I'm glad to meet you," I greeted him.

"Same for me," he replied nonchalantly, with a half-smile.

"What is your university like?" I asked.

"My university is one of the famous universities in China. Is that what you want to know?" He still showed a half smile.

"I'm not trying to flatter a student because he studies in a good university. The university is famous, but that doesn't mean every student there will become a famous person," I retorted, resentful of his sarcasm.

My aunt felt the tension rising between us. "Have you

eaten dry sticks?" She scolded him, "You seem to spit out sticks to beat her. But she is your own cousin, like a sister, and she is younger than you."

Brother Yong backed down, "O.K., I'm wrong. You're right. You women are always right because you have longer hair."

I laughed, then I asked him to tell me about the revolution in his university.

"Nothing worth talking about."

"Which side do you belong to? The 8.26 or the East Is Red?"

"None. I'm a free fighter."

"A free fighter? Free to fight anyone?"

"Free from the Cultural Revolution."

"The revolutionary doors are open for anyone." I quoted a well-known slogan. "Anyone may enter."

"Anyone? Yes, anyone but me!" He then said, "At the beginning of the revolution I joined the Red Guards. I am a Red Sort, of course. But a few months later, the Red Guard organization was accused of being conservative by the government newspapers, so I joined the 8.26, the rebel Red Guards. But in another few months, the government accused the 8.26 of being a counterrevolutionary organization. So I left the 8.26. Then in another month, the government issued the Sichuan Document, saying the arrest of the rebel Red Guards was a mistake. I applied to rejoin the 8.26. But . . ."

"But the 8.26 won't allow you in. Right?"

"Not only that. The Woman Leader of the 8.26 slapped me. She slapped me in public. And she yelled that I was just a pumpkin seed blowing about with the wind."

I couldn't help laughing at this.

He continued. "I did nothing wrong. I just followed the

government." He frowned and scratched his head.

I laughed again, this time because he looked so foolish. I changed the subject and asked him to take me to Sichuan University to have a look.

The university gate was an ancient gray stone tunnel. Past the tunnel, tall, dense French Parasol trees formed a long archway. This led to a large lotus pond, surrounded by several large playgrounds. Beyond, there were row after row of traditional Chinese pavilions, all gray with curved roofs, on which stood figures of different animals—horses, unicorns, cows, turtles and lions. I held my breath, enchanted by this evidence of the old civilization.

"This is the Department of Chinese Literature," Brother Yong announced.

"You study in such beautiful pavilions. You are very lucky. Do you have a library?"

"Sure," he said, and turned left where there was a round, tall, dark-blue pavilion. "Our library."

The library was quiet. Only a few people were there reading. We walked from floor to floor and room to room. Each floor had three large reading rooms, and each room had bookshelves. On each of the shelves was a cardboard sign that said, "Poisonous Grasses."

I sighted *Wang Gui and Li Xiang Xiang,* the popular ballad written by Li Ji, a revolutionary poet. I picked it out and nudged Brother Yong. "Why is this book called 'poisonous grass'? The author is a revolutionary who used to be a soldier in the Red Army," I whispered.

"Have you read the ballad?" he asked.

"I read it long ago. It describes the author's revolutionary life."

"Remember the two lines in the poem about love?

Stars, many, in the sky;
Grapes, many, on the vine;
I, a poor man, have only one wife.

Any book about love is a 'poisonous grass' because love is bourgeois poison."

"But that poem is a joke," I argued.

"He jokes about 'wife,' the synonym of love. Besides, nobody is allowed to joke about 'wife' or 'woman.' A professor in my department once compared a woman to a vase. My, he got criticized. After all, a Chinese woman cannot be considered a thing, like a vase, to decorate the house. Chinese women are proletarians. As the newspapers say, 'Women Hold Up Half the Sky,' right?"

"Well, then, if all those books are now considered 'poisonous grasses,' why doesn't your university burn them?" I said as we walked out.

"Keep the 'poisonous grass' for fertilizing the earth," he quoted Mao's saying, apparently joking.

"What do you mean 'for fertilizing the earth'?"

"Criticizing the 'poisonous grass' books can raise people's political awareness—that is what Chairman Mao meant."

"How high has your political awareness been raised?"

"Nearly to the sky!"

"Brother Yong, do you want to be a writer some day?"

"No. I wouldn't write about my humiliating history. I wouldn't write that I had been slapped by a woman in public."

"Is there any pretty girl in your life whom you might like to write about?"

"Do you want me to ask you if there is a handsome man in your life who likes you?"

124

"But there is, indeed, a man in my life. He is handsome, a university student."

"And he must say to you, 'many stars in the sky, many grapes on the vine, and I only have you.' Am I right? Let me tell you, there was, indeed, a pretty girl in my life."

"Where is she?" I asked.

"She is dead."

"In the war?"

"In the heart."

"Brother Yong, don't talk in riddles."

"I am serious. She died of a heart attack. She was my neighbor. She had heart disease. She wanted to marry me and I wanted to marry her. But my mother said no, because she had heart disease. My mother has a loud voice. When she said, 'No, I won't allow you to marry a sick girl, I don't want a sick girl to be my daughter-in-law!' her loud voice passed out the window and into the girl's ears. At that, her heart broke and she died."

To get to the other side of the campus we walked through a wood. I was startled to see that at the other end of the wood was a big graveyard. Brother Yong told me it was for the bodies of the students who had died in the recent armed battles. Before the graveyard stood a monument as tall as a building. On it was carved 8.26 and all the names of those belonging to that organization who had been killed. At the time Sichuan University was the bastion of the 8.26. The names of the members of the opposing faction who had been killed were not carved on the monument. Actually, many who were killed were passers-by, Yong said. Their names were not on the monument either.

Beyond the graveyard there were groups of western-style buildings. They were the Department of Foreign Languages. Every building was surrounded with flower gardens, but the gardens had few flowers. In the center of each garden was a big hole. "What are all the holes for?" I asked.

"They are air-raid shelters. In case the Guomindang troops and imperialists come to attack us."

"Are you kidding?"

"No, I swear." He raised his right hand, and declared it solemnly, "The 8.26 leaders called on us free fighters to dig those holes for shelter in case the Guomindang troops and the imperialists come to attack us."

"Called on only the free fighters? What about the other students?" I asked.

"They hide on the top of the buildings to keep a watch on Chengdu University of Communications, and they fire at each other at night."

"Many been killed?"

"Not too many because they shoot at night. They can't see clearly."

"Are there any students of the East Red staying in this school?"

"No. All of them have been driven away to Chengdu University of Communications."

"Are there any students of the 8.26 in Chengdu University of Communications?"

"No. They have moved to our university."

"Will they kill each other when they meet?"

"Sure."

"But nobody will kill you because you are a free fighter?"

"That's right."

"How many free fighters in your department?"

"Eighty-five percent. So our library is open."

"But I didn't see many of them in the library. Where are they?"

"They sleep all the time. Until they feel hungry. Then they

go to the dining halls to eat."

"How many dining halls do you have?"

"Fourteen. We have fourteen departments, and each has a dining hall."

"Does each have a library?"

"Yes. Each has a swimming pool, too. The Department of Foreign Languages has the biggest one."

"Will you tell me something more about the Department of Foreign Languages?"

"Well, that department produces beauties."

"You are kidding again."

"No, I'm serious. This department never accepted a bad-looking student. The girls in this department are most beautiful."

"Why?"

"Because after graduation they work as diplomats abroad. Their appearance represents China."

"Brother Yong, I would like to study English, but I don't know if my appearance is O.K. or not."

He half-closed his eyes and looked me up and down for a while, then said, "You might be O.K., but a little bit too short."

"I know, but I really want to study English. All the teachers said I have a talent for languages. I always got good marks in high school."

"Well, there is a way to make you taller. Go buy a pair of high-heeled shoes."

"But the Cultural Revolution doesn't allow me to wear high heels. They are called capitalist shoes."

"Let me tell you what, there is a perfect way. Learn to dance ballet so that you can walk on your toes. That will certainly make you much taller. How about that?"

"Brother Yong. I'm angry with you. You're teasing me

again. You never talk seriously." I left him and hurried back to my aunt's place.

But the next morning Brother Yong came to see me. He apologized, and brought me a little English dictionary. "I'm used to making jokes," he said. "These days life is so dull. Jokes can help."

He suggested that I visit his university again to see what the university students were like. So I climbed up on the back seat of his bicycle and we rode off. Soon we arrived at his university room. The door to the university dormitory was half open. Without knocking on the door, he entered and led me in by the hand. There were seven students in the room. Some were asleep, some playing cards, some smoking. Empty bottles were everywhere and trash was piled behind the door. There were four wooden bunk beds in the room; none of them were made up. Dirty clothes lay on the floor or hung on beds, filling the room with a strong smell of sweat.

"I brought my cousin to visit all of you, to see the university students of these times," Brother Yong announced in a mock-serious tone. Several stood up, and bowed to me, saying, "Thank you, Your Majesty." The ones in bed said, "Your Majesty, will you have mercy and close your eyes for five minutes to let us dress?"

I laughed and closed my eyes.

They made me tea. One of them suggested, "To honor Your Majesty, let's have a party right now." At this, one took out his flute and two fetched down their violins from the wall. Brother Yong said he would like to recite from Shakespeare's *Romeo and Juliet*. He asked me to perform the role of Juliet with him.

"But I can't remember the dialogue," I said.

"You are always so serious. I can't recite it either. We'll

128

just make it up. Nothing is serious around here."

They played one of the best-known Chinese folk songs, "Flowers and Boys," which describes a group of boys gazing at roses in a garden that all turn out to be beautiful girls. Then they are dancing together under the moonlight. The music was merry, and Brother Yong and I couldn't help singing along.

After that they played a very old song, "The River Is Red," which the great patriot, Yue Fei, wrote when he was in prison eight hundred years ago. He was a brilliant general who fought bravely to defend China against foreign invaders and was completely loyal to the Sung dynasty emperor, but he was wrongly accused by a treacherous prime minister so the emperor had Yue Fei arrested and executed. Since then, Yue Fei has become a people's hero, loved and respected throughout the country. When singing this song, most of those in the room cried.

For lunch we had noodles in tomato-egg soup. We cooked together in the room on a little handmade, rusty electric stove.

The young men told me that none of them would like to be a writer.

"It is the most dangerous career," one boy said, "because we have read too many poisonous books and we have been poisoned already. If we were to write, we would only write poisonous books."

I remained in Chengdu for about three months. Every day I went to read in the Sichuan University library. By the end of my stay, I had finished a great many famous works, both ancient and contemporary. In the evening I studied the English dictionary by myself.

During my stay in Chengdu my writer friend Tao Kuang wrote me a long letter. Enclosed was a copy of *Li Sao* in

129

her own handwriting. She encouraged me to write and to send my writing to her. She emphasized, "Write everything true to life." She also sent me a photograph of herself standing beside a pine tree at Gold Top Temple on Mount Emei.

I wrote back right away, and told her I was reading the so-called poisonous books and I sent her a few poems I had written in my diary.

One day in January, Brother Yong came to see me and brought great news: "The Cultural Revolution ends today!" he announced.

"Today? How?"

"A military team came to our university today and ordered all the East Red students to return to school. They told all the students to unite with each other and wait for jobs."

It was too good to be true. The Cultural Revolution ended. It was just like a dream. I was very excited. "Do you think all the universities will reopen for high school graduates soon?" I asked.

"Sure. The military men mentioned that too, at the school meeting."

I was very happy. I packed my bags immediately, and caught the night train home.

He held me tightly to him. . .

CHAPTER 12

Waiting

等 待

"Hello, it's good to see you again," Xiong, the Beijing Red Guard, greeted me as I got off the train in the morning.

"Hello, good to see you again, too," I said. "Why are you here at the station?"

"I was seeing my relative off. He is going to Chongqing."

It was a pleasant, sunny morning, and he suggested that we walk home along the river.

"Where have you been for so many months?" he asked.

"In Chengdu, with my old aunt, just for three months."

"You are lucky. You missed the tragic deaths."

"Deaths?"

"Tragic deaths. Eleven students from your school were killed."

"What?"

"They were tricked!"

"Tricked by whom?"

"By the local army," he said. "One afternoon, last month, a messenger from the local army unit came to your school to see you."

"See me?"

"Yes, because you were the leader of the ten-thousand Rebel Red Guards. He didn't find you, so he went to Yulan and Shen Min, and told them to go to the local military command building that night. He said the officers of the command were willing to supply them with guns, and that the guns were piled on the second floor of the building. That night Yulan and Shen Min led fifty students there to get the guns. But when they reached the first floor, rifles went off. Yulan was the first to be killed. Shen Min and the other nine were also killed, and the rest were badly wounded. We were all furious when we heard about this massacre, and I immediately decided to call on all the rebel Red Guards to carry the dead bodies in a parade to demonstrate against the murderers. But, then, we observed that all the high buildings, including the city theater, had machine guns and cannons set up on the roofs. The military command had also plastered the city with posters declaring, 'The Attempt to Seize Arms Is a Counterrevolutionary Crime!' We realized that if we paraded through the streets, as planned, another massacre, much bloodier and much larger, would be launched against us Red Guards. But I did go by myself to see our comrades' bodies. They were heaped left and right before the gate of the military command post. Because it had been labeled a counterrevolutionary incident, many parents never even dared to claim the bodies of their children. Those who did come to get the bodies had to hold funerals in secret because public ceremonies for counterrevolutionaries were forbidden."

Even now I cannot find words to describe how I felt at that moment. We walked along the river in silence.

After a while, Xiong continued. "Yulan's mother fainted at the funeral that we had in their house. I helped send her to the hospital. She is now in Tibet. Yulan's father came to take her there."

"Why does the local command want to kill innocent students?" I asked angrily.

"To get rid of their anger."

"About what?"

"They are angry about the Cultural Revolution. They feel the rebel Red Guards are troublemakers."

"But Chairman Mao called on us to establish the rebel Red Guards."

"I hate him—the worst emperor in Chinese history!"

"Who?" I was shocked.

"The one who launched the Cultural Revolution and tricked us into joining." He looked at me. His eyes seemed to be on fire. "The Cultural Revolution is a plot," Xiong went on bitterly. "He designed it to kick out Chairman Liu Shaoqi from the central government so that he could be in supreme power, the only emperor to control China!"

"An emperor?" at this word a chill ran through me. How could he compare Mao to a feudal emperor? Suddenly, I remembered Tao Kuang's words at Mount Emei, about the emperors in Chinese history. Did she imply Mao? I thought of the Cultural Revolution and of my friends and my teachers. Many of them were dead. They died in different periods of the Cultural Revolution because of the different policies—all of which had been issued by Mao. How could it be explained?

Xiong continued, "The Cultural Revolution is a banquet of man-eating-man, and Mao is the host!"

I tried to calm myself, tried to recall how the revolution had started, and how I had joined in. I asked him, "Do you remember the criticism of an old play, *Magistrate Hai Rui Loses His Position*, at the beginning of the Cultural Revolution? What was that for?"

"That was Mao's trick too. He muddied the waters to catch a big fish."

"Why did he have to do that?"

"Because Mao was afraid people would see through his scheme to kick Chairman Liu out of the central government."

"I don't understand. Mao can do anything he wants to. He could easily deal with Chairman Liu without launching such a big revolution, couldn't he? Every Chinese listens to Chairman Mao and does whatever he asks. Am I right?"

"No. Not completely," he said. "You must know that Chairman Liu had very high prestige in China, higher than Mao's before the Cultural Revolution."

"Higher than Mao?"

"Yes, especially in Beijing. Beijing people had very deep feelings for Liu and listened only to Liu. That was why, at the beginning of the revolution, Mao rushed to Shanghai to find his allies, Zhang Chunqiao, Yao Wenyuan, and Wang Hongwen. Then he wrote to his wife, Jiang Qing, telling her to set up the Cultural Revolution Committee of the central government in Beijing to control the revolution. That's how Jiang Qing and those three men—later known as the 'Gang of Four'—became the real power in the committee, and how they now dominate China."

"Shanghai? In August 1966?"

"Yes."

"I was in a bandit village then, working for a Socialist Education Team. I'd been there for only six weeks when I was ordered to return to school immediately. I was told all the Work Teams were dismissed by Mao. I didn't understand why."

"That was another of Mao's tricks. He used it to embarrass Chairman Liu."

"How did that embarrass Chairman Liu?"

"Because it was Liu who had sent the Work Teams to the countryside to lead the movement. You see, at the beginning, Liu didn't realize that Mao was scheming. Liu thought the Cultural Revolution was like all previous political movements, meant to deal with ordinary people. Liu was trying to contribute to the Cultural Revolution, but he fell into Mao's trap. When Mao returned to Beijing from Shanghai, he accused Liu of doing things behind his back. He also accused Liu of trying to put China on the capitalist road. That's when the new term, 'capitalist roader' was born."

The reference to capitalist roaders reminded me of the Dark February, and so I asked, "How did the Dark February happen?"

That was something the old leaders in the central government thought up. They were angry at Mao for using the revolution to try and destroy Chairman Liu. They were trying to use Dark February to jail the rebel Red Guards to stop the Cultural Revolution. But they failed. As a result Chairman Liu was put under house arrest, and his supporters in the central government were persecuted."

"How about Premier Zhou? Did he support Liu?" I asked.

"Yes. Premier Zhou is very ill. Mao is trying to get rid of him. Mao and his wife with the three men have been persecuting him secretly because they know every Chinese loves our premier."

"Who told you all of this about the Cultural Revolution?" I asked.

"My schoolmates in Beijing. No wall can hold secrets inside. Now the university students are awakening. Perhaps China can still be saved."

Then he quoted the Russian communist leader, Lenin: "The direction of university students represents the direction of society."

Suddenly, the yearning to go to university overwhelmed me. How I wished I could become one of those students. I asked, "Do you think the Cultural Revolution is ending now?"

"I don't know. How is it possible that Mao would try to end the revolution before he manages to conquer all the rebel Red Guards throughout the country?"

"What do you mean?"

"I mean Mao will use new tricks to deal with the rebel students. He is afraid of them because they are so rebellious, so wild, and they have been trained to be so strong and powerful by the revolution. After all, if they were able to overthrow Liu in the past, they will be able to overthrow Mao in the future."

"But my cousin, Brother Yong, said all the university students will get jobs soon and all the universities will reopen for high school graduates."

"It's good to hope so. I heard Mao is going to send factory workers' teams to occupy all the high schools in the cities, and peasant teams to occupy the high schools in the countryside. To send such political teams is Mao's old way of suppressing people, to shut the mouths of intellectuals."

"When are you returning to your university then?" I asked.

"Not until I have learned how to practice qigong."

"What for?"

138

"For self-protection. I have to prepare myself. I could be sent to jail again. You know, when I was in jail during the Dark February, they threw stools at my head. They are damned monsters. Recently I read a book that says if you master qigong nobody will be able to hurt you."

Xiong continued. "So many friends have been killed by this revolution. Tan Wen was killed in Chongqing."

"Tan Wen? The Red Guard from Chengdu Industrial University?" I was surprised.

"Yes. It happened two months ago. He was shot in Chongqing. They recognized him as an important student leader of Chengdu and kidnapped him. They shot him that night in Sa Pin Ba, the suburb of Chongqing, together with seven other rebel Red Guards. Tan Wen's mother went to Chongqing and wailed in the streets for help for three days."

I couldn't bear to hear any more. He began to smoke. He was a short man and the smoke filled my nose. Fortunately, my home was within view now—it was already noon—and I said goodbye.

On my desk at home I saw a thick letter from Tao Kuang. She had read my poems and liked them. She told me that to write a poem was like creating a painting. "Imagine yourself a painter, and describe everything as pictures in colors that embody your feelings." She also told me, "A great book is made by writing the truth. A great author is an honest person. Write the things you feel. Write them down honestly, because life itself is honest." She encouraged me to keep writing diaries every day, and said, "writing is the most serious pursuit. A writer is a sculptor of the human soul. We have a great responsibility to our readers." The poems I had sent to her were enclosed in the letter. She had made many suggestions about them in the margins.

She said she liked my "Boats" very much:

> The river is sleepy under stars,
> Two boats are sighing, on each bank.
> "Go to bed now?" one boat asks.
> "No, I'm worried," the other replies.

The next morning I went to school, where I received three letters and a package from Deng He. In the first letter he told me that during the last months there had been violent, bloody fighting at his school. Two different Red Guard groups fought each other all the time. Since they were military students, they possessed pistols and rifles, and each was an expert shot. One night Deng He's group was holding a party. He with twenty others were performing on the school stage. Somehow the other group stole in and shot at the performers. Deng He had jumped behind the big wooden column on the stage and so was not hurt. The shell that came near only knocked off his hat. But nine of his schoolmates were killed. "Little Devil," he wrote, "I miss you so much, especially after that incident. God let me live because he knows I love you. Let me see you. I want to see you so much, right now."

The date on the letter indicated it had been written a month ago. I wondered why the school hadn't forwarded it to my home. I opened the package. This contained a mug, a white towel and schoolbag. The schoolbag contained a pen and diary of his, in which he had written that he loved me. I was very touched.

The two more recent letters told me he was in a happy mood again. He said Marshal Lin Biao, Chairman of the Military Committee of the central government, was going to be Chairman Mao's successor, and might give the military students special preference. He was confident that he would get a good position soon. He also told me secret news he had heard from the children of high-ranking officials in his academy—that all the high school graduates would get jobs or the opportunity to study in universities. He was sure that I would be sent to one of the best.

The shadow that the conversation with Xiong had cast on me now disappeared. I was happy again. Perhaps the terrible deaths were a single incident, an isolated tragedy that would never happen again. Perhaps Xiong misunderstood the situation. Perhaps he was too one-sided, too pessimistic, I thought. I wanted to believe that Deng He was correct, that life would become peaceful and happy again, and that I would now finally go to a university. Walking through the school playground I heard the birds singing a happy song. The sun was shining. It was a cheerful day. Teachers were chatting and some were washing clothes. None of them were writing posters. What a peaceful lively picture—no politics. The Cultural Revolution had ended, I was certain.

Teacher Liu, our music teacher, was pregnant. She turned to me, smiling as I passed, and said, "The weather is beautiful, isn't it?" I smiled back. It was good to see my teachers so relaxed again.

I believed that I would become a university student at any moment, and began imagining myself sitting in a classroom at Beijing. Oh how wonderful it was to be a university student. At last, I had the opportunity. I thought of Deng He, and how I was never brave enough to tell that I loved him because I was no university student. Now I can say it to him. I have the right now because I am equal to him. It was so good to be equal to a man I deeply loved. "Deng He, my dear Deng He, I love you." I said this again and again to myself. "Deng He, I love you very, very much.

Oh, how I love you."

I decided to invite Deng He to my home to see my parents. I wanted to tell them that I loved him. It was time for me to share my secret with them. I didn't want to hide my feelings any more. Now, I was completely myself.

I went to an expensive shop to buy a gift for Deng He. I found a white silk handkerchief. It was as white as snow, the symbol of purity.

After supper I unfolded the handkerchief carefully on my desk, and with a fine pen brush wrote him a poem:

> Difficult to tell you what is in my mind.
> Ask the moon.

On a corner of the handkerchief I embroidered a pair of Mandarin Ducks, a symbol of love.

Three days later Deng He came. It was a sunny afternoon. He looked energetic, and very handsome. Standing beside him I found I came up only to his shoulders. How I wished I were taller, to match him better. I introduced him to my parents, and they seemed to like him. At the dinner table they asked him about his family, his school, and his hobbies. My father was pleased to know that he didn't smoke.

After dinner, with my parent's permission, Deng He and I went out to walk by the river. At my suggestion we went to the boat house of my uncle, a fisherman who lived alone. He had two boats, one kept in the river for fishing and the other sitting on the bank as a house.

My uncle was so happy to see us that his tanned face seemed to shine with his smile. He asked us to drink rice wine with fried peanuts which he cooked himself. He showed us his fish bird, too, a large cormorant, black as a crow, with a long beak to pick up the fish. "His name is

Meow Meow, my best friend and my money-maker. He helps me catch good fish. He dives into the river and picks up fish for me with his beak." My uncle patted the bird's back. After a while, he excused himself, telling us he was going to visit his friends. I suspect he realized we wanted to be alone with each other. "I'll leave my Meow Meow with you," he said and left.

We went out on the river in the fishing boat. The moon was mirrored in the river, a curved moon. It was yellow. The waves gently rocked the boat; the water was deep blue.

I asked Deng He to close his eyes, then I put the silk handkerchief in his hand. "A gift for you," I whispered, and he hugged me. "Thank you," he murmured. "You are the most beautiful girl in the world. I love you. Nobody can ever separate us."

I felt my eyes grow moist and tears began to run down my cheeks. I didn't know why. He held me very tight and I heard his heart beating.

When I returned home that night my stomach was aching. I became worried that I was pregnant. When the pain grew worse I decided to report it to father, even though he had already gone to bed.

"Father, I think I am pregnant."

"What?"

"I think I'm pregnant because my stomach aches so badly."

"With him?"

"Yes."

"Did you have sex before?"

"What is sex?"

My father looked embarrassed. Then he asked me, "What did he do with you?"

"He hugged me."

"When?"

"Two hours ago."

"How did he hug you? I mean, did he take off his clothes or something like that."

"No, it was cold in the boat."

My father smiled, and said, "Go to bed, you are not pregnant. But remember, never let any man hug you."

CHAPTER 13

Bad News

灾 难

On October 1, 1967, National Day, Comrade Lin Biao made a big speech at a grand celebration in Beijing. He declared: "The Chinese Cultural Revolution is the greatest revolution in the history of the communist movement. It is the new development of Chairman Mao's genius in the creation of Marxism and Leninism." On October 25, the local newspaper headlined that all students must return to school immediately. I walked to school that day, believing that the school would assign us jobs and send me to a good university.

At ten o'clock the school emergency bell rang, directing teachers and students to line up on the playground in front of the presentation platform. Then thirteen factory workers marched onto the platform. One of them, a young woman with messy hair, took the microphone and shouted into it: "First of all, let us wish our great leader, Chairman Mao, a long, long life. Let us bow to Chairman Mao, our beloved Old Man, three bows." She turned around to face a wall with a giant photo of Chairman Mao between the red flags of the People's Republic of China and the Chinese Communist Party. "And let's bow to our great leader's closest friend, Comrade Lin Biao, three bows. Wish him good health, wish him good health forever." She led the bows.

When she turned around she started lecturing: "Today, we workers have really lifted our heads because Chairman Mao has sent us onto the educational stage to be the masters of the intellectuals. From now on, all of you, including your principal and the school party secretary, must listen to us." At this the student audience stirred.

Someone on my right whispered, "That is Zi Guang's sister. She has a mental problem so the factory sent her out here." I was sorry to hear that because Zi Guang was a very bad student in my class. He was a bully who beat classmates, often those who were not strong, and we had held many class meetings to try to help him. He was from a blacksmith family, and his father was famous for making good knives. Looking around, I saw Suansuan. But as soon as her eyes met mine, she turned her head away.

The teachers were quiet. Then the young woman worker continued: "We are going to set up an organization called: The Revolutionary Committee to Lead the Revolution in the School. Of course, our Workers' Team is the majority in the committee, but we need one student and one teacher to join it. Now, go to your classrooms to elect them by secret ballot."

Teacher Wei and I were elected as the teacher and student representatives. The woman worker came to my class and asked me to fill out a form. The next day, however, when we went to school, we found no workers around. A week later the team was completely gone. Rumor had it that the factory had refused to pay their salaries because they had not shown up at the factory for days. So that was the end of that "revolutionary committee."

Again, we stayed at home, waiting.

Linlin came to visit me one evening and suggested I practice singing. She said my natural voice was good and introduced me to Xi Yi, a famous singer in the city theater. Xi Yi was a warm person and immediately agreed to teach me.

"Your voice is sweet," she said, "but not strong. So first you'll have to learn how to breathe. A strong voice comes from strong breath." She led me over to a flower pot in the room, saying, "Try to breathe all the fragrance into your stomach." Next she taught me to imitate a dog barking. "Thus, your stomach muscles will become very strong. That is the foundation for producing a beautiful voice."

I often went to study with Xi Yi. She was a wonderful teacher. Gradually we became good friends, and she felt free to tell me things about people in the theater. One time she told me about the young dancer, Yang Yu. "Her famous dance is The Fish. She moves her arms like the fins of fish swimming in the water. But she has trouble. She married a jobless man who had lied to her about being a university student. He saw her dancing only one time, and then wrote to her every day. He is a good-looking fellow. He looks like the Russian poet Pushkin."

"I heard Yang Yu was in love with Chang Wen, the young painter," I said.

"True. Yang Yu did love him, but she left him because the painter came from a capitalist family. His father had had five wives. He was the son of the fifth wife. His family is terrible, isn't it? Who will marry him? His family background will bring problems to his children and grandchildren. You know, marrying a man from that kind of a family is like jumping into fire, burning your future."

"But I think he would be much better than that jobless man, especially since the one she married lied to her. Yang Yu should have divorced him."

"Don't say that. If a woman divorces her husband it means she destroys her future with her own hands."

"I don't understand."

"People will laugh at her, and talk behind her back because she has no husband."

"She can find another husband."

"No one will marry a divorced woman. A woman who loses her husband, loses her reputation. A woman without reputation has nothing. She's lost everything."

"I don't understand."

"You know Mrs. Cai, the woman who used to be the first director of our theater? She divorced her husband because she caught him having sex with the baby sitter. She reported this to the local government, and he was arrested and sentenced to eight years in prison. After that she herself lost her position as director and was branded as a relative of a reactionary.

"Reactionary?"

"Yes, because her husband was in jail. Anyone who is in jail is a reactionary."

"But she had divorced him. She is no longer his relative."

"She is—because she is the children's mother."

That night I thought much about divorce for women and felt very sorry for Mrs. Cai. But what was sex? It must be something very serious. I decided to go ask Linlin's mother about it.

Weeks went by, I spent much time practicing singing, and my voice greatly improved. I was pleased and said to myself nothing was too difficult so long as one tried and kept trying.

One day military teams arrived in our city to lead the revolutionary movement of every unit. But within a week, all the teams disappeared. Rumors had it that they had been on Chairman Liu's side. Later on, new military teams arrived. There were eleven in my mother's working unit, and thirteen in my father's. And a new workers' team marched into my school. But a few days later they, too, disappeared. Nobody knew where they came from or who they were.

In April, 1968, Tao Kuang wrote me a short note:

My Dear Young Friend,

My fiance and I are in danger. Do not write to me until I write to you. Don't worry about us. We are ready to go through it. "Lilies stay clean even though they grow in muddy waters." We are prepared to sit in jail for the rest of our lives.

Be brave. Keep writing. It is not for me, for you, but for the world.

Tao Kuang

I heeded Tao Kuang. I wrote down everything I experienced in my diary. I studied the English dictionary diligently too, and sometimes I wrote my diaries in English. I forced myself to remember ten new words a day, although I couldn't pronounce them correctly.

For a whole month I didn't hear from Deng He. He must be sick, I thought, and to try to comfort him, I drew him a large garden of lovely roses and colorful butterflies. But I didn't receive a response after I sent it to him. He must be away on some business, I thought, believing that he would write again soon. But when months passed and I received no word from him, I believed he was dead. There was a Christian church in the western end of the city which had been closed since the beginning of the Cultural Revolution. I went there in the evenings, stood outside and prayed for Deng He. I had never believed in God before, but now I wished there was a God so that he could comfort Deng He's soul.

My parents became quieter, and one night before I went to bed, mother came into my room to tell me that father was in trouble.

"Why, mother?" I asked.

"He is accused of being a Guomindang spy by the latest military team in his work unit."

"He had nothing to do with the Guomindang."

"They said he had worked for a Guomindang factory before Liberation in 1949."

"Everyone worked for the Guomindang at that time. That was before the Communist Party took over China."

"They also said that your father had joined the city war because he wanted to take a gun home to kill communists."

"What else are they accusing him of?"

"They said he shouted a counterrevolutionary slogan: 'Long Live the Guomindang.'"

"Ridiculous!" I jumped up and went out to see Lawyer Lin. Although the court had been closed since the outbreak of the Cultural Revolution, I believed he could be of some help.

Lawyer Lin urged me to be calm.

"But they might send my father to jail. I am very worried."

"Do not worry," he said. "Tell your father not to say a word about the slogan, no matter how they threaten him. Everything will be all right."

"You mean he should say 'no'?"

"No, I mean he must not utter a single word. Tell your father to pretend to be dumb."

"If they beat him?"

"He'll just have to suffer it. The most important thing is you must tell your father to be dumb. Then everything will be all right."

"Why should the military team turn their spearheads against my father, an honest man?"

Lawyer Lin patted my shoulder and said, "After the emperor's fight, the poor folks clean up the mess." He quoted the ancient proverb, "Your father is just one of the folks."

"But they have no right to label my father a 'Guomindang Spy.'"

"The emperor," he said, "trying to redirect the people's hatred of the Cultural Revolution, has formulated the lie that 'The Guomindang's spies stirred up all the turmoil.'"

"You mean Mao?"

He didn't answer.

After a pause he said, "China has a lot of problems. One is that the laws have no authority. They are just words on pieces of paper. In our country it's always been just one man in control. Only what he says counts. If he says someone is bad, that someone is executed with no questions asked."

When I got home I told father Lawyer Lin's advice.

The next afternoon father dragged himself home, looking pale. "The military team has ordered me to attend a class- struggle meeting tomorrow morning," he told me. "The leader of the team said I must confess in front of four hundred people."

"Pretend to be dumb," I reminded him of Lawyer Lin's words.

"I feel disgraced. All the people will think I am a Guomindang spy."

Mother came over with a pair of scissors in her hand. "Let me cut the hair on your head short. I will cut it very short. I know they will pull your hair at the meeting. They do this all the time. I won't let them hurt you."

Father looked even worse the next morning. He hadn't slept all night. Mother served him breakfast, but he had no appetite.

"Eat," my mother said. But he didn't even try to touch the food.

"Father, please eat," I urged. "I will go with you to your work unit."

At father's unit he and I sat on benches in the lobby. As others arrived, I stood and greeted them: "Hello, good morning, Uncle Li. How are you doing this morning Aunt Liu?" Some of them returned my smile, but most of them ignored me. I pretended I didn't see the military team when they arrived in uniform. I held my father's hands. I wanted them to know I loved my father very much.

Father followed the team into the Struggle Meeting Hall, and I saw him to the door. Although I was locked out, I could hear the assembled participants shout, "Down with the Guomindang spy!" "Long live the Communist Party!" There were at least four hundred of them.

The struggle meeting was finished at noon, and when I was able to see my father again, I went up to him and held his hands, and then we went home for lunch.

My mother was anxiously waiting at the door, "How was it?" she asked as we came in.

"I didn't say a word," father replied.

"Did they beat you?"

"No, but they will. They will beat me this afternoon. The military team leader told me I must confess by two o'clock today."

Mother started setting the table, she had prepared chicken soup, especially for him. But before we started eating, father said he had a headache.

He rose to leave and stumbled. Mother and I rushed to support him, and helped him to his bed. He closed his eyes, his two hands clutching the edges of the bed. He spoke in a weak voice. "The house is shaking. The bed is turning over."

Mother ran out to get a doctor, while I sat beside my father. About two o'clock, seven members of the military team barged into our house.

I tried to calm myself and said, "Thank you for coming to see my father. He is very ill." They ignored me, but went to the bed and shouted to father, "You must come to the struggle meeting tomorrow morning."

The doctor arrived, checked father, and gave his diagnosis: "Meniere's syndrome." Before writing a prescription, however, the doctor asked father, "What's your class background?" I quickly answered, "A worker. Our family background is working class." At that time a doctor was not allowed to make out a prescription to a supposed Guomindang spy.

Father stayed in bed for three weeks, taking the prescribed medicines three times a day. In the fourth week I accompanied him to his work unit and there we learned that the military team had gone and a new one had taken its place. The new team ordered father to write his personal history from age seven to the present. Two weeks later, the leader of the team transferred father to a wood factory to be a carpenter. As a carpenter, father's job was to wade barefoot into cold water to pull logs out and take them to the saw.

When Lawyer Lin heard that my father had become a

carpenter, he said to me, "He is safe now."

"You mean no more political problems?"

"Right."

"Do you know why they have to put my father in that factory?"

"To save face," he said. "The situation is embarrassing for them because they failed to find anything against your father."

During this period mother and I grew closer than we had ever been before. She said I was smart and had helped father in a bright way. One night we had a chat.

"Mother," I said, "at the beginning you called the Cultural Revolution a game, and you never joined it. So, no trouble ever befell you."

"I met with big trouble," she replied. "Two military men from your father's unit came to my unit three times to try to force me to divorce your father."

"You didn't tell him, did you?"

"No. That was when he was sick in bed. How could I pour oil on the flames?"

Then she said, "Your father has been fooled by the Cultural Revolution."

"Me too," I replied.

"Anyhow, we are lucky. At least we are all alive. Look at the neighbors. Some have lost a father, some lost a mother, and many have lost children."

One day in the fall, to my great surprise, I received a note from Deng He. Deng He was alive! It seemed impossible. He wrote that he was coming to see me. I read the note again and again and checked the date. He is alive. Oh, how wonderful. Deng He is alive. Deng He is alive. This was everything to me, and I wrote him immediately asking him to come to me as soon as possible. When I put my letter in the mailbox, I realized he hadn't written to me for seven months. He must have been sick, I thought, or might have been injured in an accident. Maybe he had lost an arm or a leg. But I said to myself, "No matter what has happened to him, I love him. I will tell him I love him and I will marry him. I will spend my whole life taking good care of him."

Deng He came on Saturday afternoon. He looked perfectly healthy. I examined him from head to toe. He didn't smile, and he looked away from me.

We drank tea silently, and I knew something had gone wrong. A thought floated into my head: "He wants to break up our relationship." I tried to calm myself and I asked, "Deng He, what is on your mind? Please let me know."

He raised his eyes to mine. The expression was pleading. He said in a low voice, "I got a job in Chongqing City, a radar engineer." There was silence. "I heard that all the high school students must leave the city and go to the countryside, to become permanent peasants.

I stared at him.

"So, we can only be ordinary friends from now on," he said, his voice trembling.

My heart was crying. But I didn't let my tears out. I stood up and said, "Please, leave this house."

They arranged for us to meet at the train station.

CHAPTER 14

Running Away

生 活

I was taken to the hospital and, after two weeks of observation and tests, the doctors concluded I was suffering from a severe stomach disorder caused by emotional strain. I couldn't eat. When I tried to drink water, I vomited. They warned my parents that I might have a mental breakdown.

Deng He had deserted me. He had a right to do whatever he wanted, but I felt hurt. I felt very hurt. Life seemed too unfair to me. It wasn't just Deng He. In my semi-consciousness I realized that my bitterness encompassed much more.

Time passed slowly, and gradually I recovered. I tried to forget the past and to change myself into another person, one who realized she had to live with reality.

On November 2, 1968, all the government newspapers announced the decision made by the Ninth Congress of the Chinese Communist Party: "The Congress agrees to expel Liu Shaoqi from the Party and the government forever." Then all the newspapers called Lin Biao "our beloved Vice Chairman," "Chairman Mao's closest friend and best student." Soon there were a great many stories about Lin's revolutionary career appearing in the newspapers. One said, "it is Comrade Lin Biao, who led the greatest workers movement in Chinese history, the An Yuan Workers Strike, before the Liberation." In fact, that strike was led by Liu Shaoqi. But nobody seemed to be willing to argue with the newspapers at the time. There were many facts that needed to be disputed in the Cultural Revolution. The newspapers also described Lin as a super being, "Our Vice Chairman Lin Biao is a Tian Ma (Heavenly Horse). He can fly in the sky without any difficulty." The newspapers also praised him as a genius, saying he brilliantly developed Mao Zedong's thoughts, especially his military philosophy.

In late December of that year, the government announced that all high school students must go to the countryside to become peasants. According to this policy, the countryside was a big school and the peasants would be the teachers. We were ordered to return to school to get our village assignments.

At the school meeting I saw the teachers, who were back from the concentration camps. They looked tense. The Communist Party Secretary read the policy declaration: "To go to the countryside is Chairman Mao's greatest strategy for the Cultural Revolution. We must mobilize all students to go there, to receive re-education from the peasants. The countryside is the only place for students to develop their abilities and talents and make themselves useful. We must make the mobilization a big event, and everybody must join in."

After this reading, the party secretary asked us to discuss

the far-reaching significance of this policy. No students listened to him, and we all went home.

Rage welled up in me. "Mao tricked us, and I won't let him trick me again." I told myself over and over. "I won't go to the countryside. I will not go."

That evening two teachers came to my home to mobilize me. "Sorry," I said. "I was just leaving." And I left the house.

The next evening they came again, and I again excused myself. The third evening they stopped me and explained they had been given the task by the school to convince me to be the first to go to the countryside. They said, "You are a student leader. Your action commands the others. If you won't go, we will be punished."

"How?" I asked.

"In the cowshed, the concentration camp."

"I thought you had been freed."

"No, we are allowed out only to talk the young people into going to the countryside to become peasants."

To be polite, my parents served them tea. My mother comforted them, "Everyone has problems. I understand your problem, but we need a little more time. My daughter has just returned from the hospital, where she stayed for many weeks. She is still very weak. We don't want to see her die, do we? She is your good student, and she is my daughter. Let's take a little time about this."

That night I heard my parents talking. My mother was worried. "I don't know if she will be able to cope with this new trouble or not. This is another big political movement, seems very forceful. I was really scared seeing her in the hospital. She almost died. I don't understand why she got so sick, just because of a man. I thought she was brave."

My father said, "She is brave and intelligent, but too

emotional."

I stayed at home practicing singing, reading my English dictionary, and writing in my diary. I tried to keep as busy as possible.

In February, 1969, the first group of students was mobilized. They were put in twenty-three trucks lined up on the main street. The trucks were decorated with red-paper flowers and ribbons. All the students wore red-paper flowers on their left arms.

On the trees and walls of shops hung a great many brightly colored paper streamers with political slogans: "To go to the countryside is glorious!" "To go to the countryside is a great joy!" "To go to the countryside is Chairman Mao's greatest, wisest, and most correct strategy! This strategy will make it certain that China maintains the communist red color for a million years!"

Both sides of the street were packed with people, mostly parents, seeing off their children in the trucks. They had smiles on their faces, but every once in a while someone would secretly wipe away a tear.

Suddenly I heard a voice calling me. It was Suansuan! She was in one of the trucks. "Suansuan!" I called and ran through the crowd toward her.

I stood on my toes and stretched out my arms to try to reach Suansuan's hands; my eyes blurred. Suansuan leaned over the side of the truck, trying to reach me. She was crying. A policeman separated us, saying "The truck is leaving."

The truck was moving. All the trucks were moving. Soon, they were gone, leaving behind thick dust. I didn't know how long I stood on the street. When I came back to myself, I felt as if I were standing somewhere I never knew.

That evening I went to look for Suansuan's mother, and

I finally found her living in a small brick shed. The floor was cement. Suansuan's mother had changed completely. Her hair had turned all gray, and her face was wrinkled and small. "I saw Suansuan in the truck," I said. "Why did you let her go to the countryside to be a peasant?"

She didn't speak.

"I won't go. I will fight it to the end." I told her.

She ran her hand through her hair, and said slowly, "You and Suansuan both should have studied in universities. Reality is cruel. To fight reality is to throw an egg against the wall. Suansuan's father was stoned to death."

"Suansuan's father?" I couldn't believe it.

"Yes, in a struggle meeting, he resisted them," she said, without any expression on her face. "They ordered him to confess."

"Confess what?"

"Confess that he was from a landlord family, and that they were Buddhists."

"When did it happen? Why didn't Suansuan tell me?"

"In August, 1966, when Suansuan came back from a commune."

I felt guilty to hear this. That was when Suansuan had called me an opportunist and since then we hadn't spoken. Suansuan, please forgive me. How I wished I could have done something for you.

The political situation in our city grew more and more intense. All parents were required to attend special meetings in their work units and in the streets. They were told to send their children to the countryside. Otherwise, their salaries would be stopped.

On April 1, 1969, a second group of students was mobilized and thirty-two decorated trucks carried them away. Then a third group was sent to the countryside. On

April 10, 1969, the Ninth National Congress of the Chinese Communist Party in Beijing announced the new party constitution. The constitution confirmed Lin Biao as Mao's "close comrade-in-arms and successor."

In May, a fourth group was sent away, and in June, a fifth. I stayed at home.

Every evening the street leaders visited my house. So did the work unit leaders and the schoolteachers. Mother began to cough. She was exhausted from dealing with such a situation. And she had to look after my father, who now suffered badly from rheumatism because of his daily work in cold water.

One day mother coughed up blood. Father and I both became worried. I felt I had to leave home, otherwise the endless political visits would kill her.

Every evening I went for a long walk, trying to think of a way out. And one evening, just as I was leaving the house, Linlin arrived.

"I came to tell you something very important," she said. When I took her into my bedroom, she carefully bolted the door. "I met two men today in the street. They came from the Xikang Asbestos Mine to search for talented girls to join in their mine theater. They chose me."

"How did they know you are talented?"

"I don't know. They just stopped me and asked if I was a high school student. After I answered, they asked me if I could dance or sing songs. I told them I danced ballet. Then they took me to their hotel lobby and asked me to dance. I did, and they accepted me and said they will take me to the mine tomorrow. I recommended you to them because they need a singer."

"Good for you! Of course I'll go." I was excited. "Linlin, take me to that hotel. I want to see them right now."

At the hotel we met the workers, dressed casually. They looked like honest people to me. They asked me to sing and, when I finished singing a popular song, they wrote down my name and accepted me into their mine theater. They asked both of us to keep this to ourselves; otherwise, they said, all of us might be arrested and accused of disrupting the "Go to the Countryside Movement."

"Where is the mine?" I asked.

"A border area near Tibet."

"Will you really supply us with food?" I asked.

"Yes. We will supply your food, room and pay each of you twenty yuan a month."

"Twenty yuan?" Linlin said happily.

"Yes, our mine is rich, and kind of independent from the state."

"How can it be independent from the state?" I asked.

"Because the mine is located in a minority area, and its workers are mostly Yi people. The government gives priority to minority nationalities. It's part of the policy of 'Respect for the Minorities.'"

They arranged for us to meet them the next day at the Chengdu railway station seventy-five miles away. They told us to take the first train at nine o'clock in the morning.

To leave home without letting my parents know was not easy. For one thing, mother and I shared a chest of drawers where all my clothes were and this was usually locked. She kept the key in her pocket, so the only time I could get it without her knowing would be at night when she was a-sleep. A bigger problem was the city resident book, a booklet every city family had, in which I was officially identified as a city member. If the neighborhood committee leaders crossed my name off this booklet, I would automatically be considered a permanent peasant belonging to the countryside and I would never again be allowed to become a resident of a city.

When I arrived home, my mother lay in a bed in my room. She slept there so her cough wouldn't wake my sick father. I pretended I was very tired and went to bed. In a few minutes I pretended to snore, and my mother switched off her light. As soon as I heard her snoring, I got up and went to the chair where she had laid her pants. In the pocket, I found her string of keys. In the dark it was difficult to find the right key among the many on the string. I tried them one by one until I had it and unlocked the chest. I remembered exactly where my clothes were placed in the chest along with my mother's. It was so dark I had to feel the material carefully to tell mine from hers. When I had finally gathered all my clothes for the four seasons, I put them under my pillow and quilt and lay down. That night I didn't sleep a wink.

The next morning, I stayed in bed until my parents went out to work. Then I got up, quickly washed and ate some bread while packing. By eight-thirty I was ready to go except for one thing: finding a place to hide the city resident book. At last I decided to hide it in my mother's boot. That way she would be sure to know that she must do something to keep my name from being deleted from the city register. Finally, I wrote a note to my parents, "I am leaving."

At the bus stop I saw Linlin. To avoid drawing attention to ourselves we merely nodded to each other, then stepped onto the bus separately. The bus arrived at the train station. As I headed to the station office to buy the tickets, Linlin stopped me, saying, "Let me buy the ticket for you this time, since you bought one for me to Mount Emei."

"Where did you get the money?" I asked. She didn't answer. "Did you tell your mother about this? Did she give you the money?"

"Yes."

"But you are not supposed to tell anybody. We swore not to."

"I had to tell my mother," Linlin explained in a low voice. "I cannot go away without telling her. Mother won't tell anyone else. She loves me. If I didn't let her know where I was, she would die."

"O.K., let it be. Everybody loves you. You don't know how beautiful you are," I joked, as we boarded the train. Because I had not slept all night I now felt very sleepy. But Linlin was not. She kept asking: "Do you really believe the two men will treat us well?"

"Linlin, don't worry. Even if there is a mountain of knives ahead, I will carry you on my back and cross over it. There is no way back."

The train moved slowly, and I felt sleepier. Linlin said, "I wish you were a man, not a woman."

"Why?"

"If you were a man, I would marry you. You are so brave."

I opened my eyes, and looked at Linlin, a beautiful young woman. She was holding her long hair, smiling at me. Tears came to my eyes. Linlin, such an innocent, sweet woman, such a talented, kindhearted woman, deserved to be loved by every one. She deserved to be married to the best husband. However, she only hoped to marry someone because he was brave. Having lived in such insecurity for so long since her father was put in jail, Linlin needed protection. "I will do my best to protect her, I will do everything I can to make her happy," I said to myself.

To chase away the sadness, I said, "Linlin, do you know what the difference is between a man and a woman? I mean, do you know how a man makes a woman pregnant?"

"Of course I know. It's a chair. A man sits in a chair. It becomes warm. If a woman sits in that warm chair, she becomes pregnant."

"No. Let me tell you, it's something very funny, very uncivilized." Then I told her.

"Who told you that?" she said with great surprise.

"Your mother," I said.

At the Torch Festival Yi boys and girls meet. . .

CHAPTER 15

At the Asbestos Mines

石棉矿

When the train arrived at Chengdu in the late afternoon, the two men from the asbestos mine were waiting at the station. They took us to their truck and we drove to the Chengdu Paper Factory where they said the mine theater actors and actresses were staying.

As the truck stopped, all the actors and actresses came out to cheer. There were over a hundred of them. The director of the mine theater informed us that they had given performances in many factories in Chengdu during the past several weeks, but were returning to the mine the next evening. After we took showers, the director brought us white silk shirts, blue silk skirts, cashmere sweaters, and wool flannel coats. "Your uniforms," he said. And he gave each of us twenty yuan.

The dinner was a feast of nine courses and soup. After dinner, we held a party. Every one sang, danced and laughed. Linlin was extremely happy. I was too. Overnight, life seemed to have changed from hell to heaven.

The next day, while the others were busy packing, Linlin and I walked around because we didn't have much to pack. The factory was large but empty. A few workers were smoking outdoors and some women were chatting. We came to the back gate and found it open. From the gate we saw the countryside and a stream. We went out to the stream to see people fishing. A young fisherman told me he worked in the paper factory. "Nobody works in the factory?" I asked him.

"No," he said.

"How do you make a living then?"

"The government feeds us."

"And pays you a monthly salary?"

"Absolutely."

"But you don't work."

"The government pays us, anyway."

"Why?"

"These are revolutionary times."

"I hope the peasants don't stop working in the fields or all of China will starve," I said.

"They did stop for months. Heard of the slogan, 'It is better to waste the communist fields than to plow a capitalist land'?"

"It's just a slogan," I said. "I can't believe the peasants stopped working. If they had, all the city people would have been starving."

"Many cities are starving. That's why Comrade Mao Zedong ordered all the high school students to the country-side. So the government won't have to feed them!"

Linlin did not join in our conversation. She just gazed down at her reflection in the water. She always tried to avoid political talk. She was afraid her family background would get her into trouble, no matter what she said or did.

Around ten o'clock in the evening we boarded a large, comfortable bus that took us to the asbestos mines. In the bus, the director showed us where the refreshments were, telling us to help ourselves. He said, "The asbestos mines are beyond the famous Ni Bar Shan mountain in Xikang. You'll be on the bus for seventeen hours."

We began moving gently through the lighted Chengdu, and soon we were on the dark road leading toward Tibet. Someone turned on a radio and light music floated through the vehicle, like a lullaby, soothing everyone to sleep. In my daze, the past, the present, and the future surrounded me, taking me somewhere, I didn't know. I felt I was caught in a wheel being spun around by a magician's hand.

When I woke up the next morning, the bus had stopped on a bleak mountain road. Wild grass, dead and dry, and as tall as a man, was on both sides of the road. As the wind ruffled through the grass, I caught sight of row after row of little white grave stones. History told me this area had been a famous battlefield two thousand years ago, when twenty thousand peasant warriors were killed in a fierce battle against the royal army of Emperor Qin Shihuang.

We got off and rested on the road. It was quiet; nobody was talking, and the place seemed to be dead. But then Linlin stood up and went to chase a butterfly. Her beauty moved me, and suddenly I felt the land come back to life.

About two o'clock in the afternoon, we reached Ni Bar Shan Mountain. We got off to have lunch at the inn at the foot of the mountain. I tried to see to the peak, but couldn't. It was too high in the clouds.

The bus moved up very slowly. Linlin became nervous. She told me that her heart was dropping. I felt sick too, but

171

I didn't admit it. Instead, I told her a funny story. "Did you know," I said, "in the Qin Dynasty each emperor had nine thousand concubines? Most of them lived their whole lives deep in the imperial palace, never having a chance to see the emperor. But some ambitious concubines knew how to bribe eunuchs in the emperor's chambers. They gave the eunuchs gifts or money so that the eunuchs would ask painters to draw beautiful pictures of them to show to the emperor. In that way, they met the emperor. Some of them later became empresses."

Linlin still seemed nervous, and kept looking out the window. "Linlin, do you remember the Elephant Temple on Mount Emei? There is a tale about it. Long, long ago the mountain was controlled by monsters and devils who put the area into eternal night. The people suffer and a young man resolves to walk up to the mountaintop to make a plea to Heaven. He prays as he walks and on the forty-ninth day he finally reaches the top. He sees a large cloud of seven colors above his head. On the cloud there is an old man wearing a square purple hat, riding a white elephant. The elephant has seven long tusks. He runs to follow the clouds down the mountain and when he is blocked by a pond he finds the cloud and the old man both gone. At the same time, the darkness of the area has also disappeared. Beside the pond he sees a clear trace of elephant's tracks. 'This must be Buddha Pushu who has heard my prayer and come down from Heaven to save the people,' he exclaims. Everyone is thankful to the Buddha Pushu and builds him a temple, the Elephant Temple."

Linlin interrupted, "There are two houses on each side of the Elephant Temple and each has seven little rooms without windows. What are they?"

"They are the Cleanliness and Treasure Pavilions, but

people called them the 'Beget-Sons Halls.' Know why? Ninety-five percent of the young, healthy women who slept in there for just one night got pregnant. The young palace monks pretended that they were gods sent from heaven to sleep with the women."

Linlin giggled and now looked completely relaxed. "Say, you said in history each emperor had nine thousand women concubines. Well, how many men-concubines could a woman emperor have?" she asked.

"An empress is allowed to have only two male concubines . . ." We went on like this until we finally arrived at the asbestos mines, and the bus stopped.

"Big mountains!" Linlin exclaimed. We found ourselves surrounded by ranges and ranges of huge mountains. I felt we had changed into little people. Even when I spoke in normal tones I could hear my voice echoing in the distance.

"All the mountains are asbestos mountains," the director told us, "and the miners work inside."

"How many mines are here?" I asked with excitement.

"Ten," he said. "Each has a club, a playground, and a dining hall."

"All are underground?"

"Yes." The director smiled and pointed to two four-story buildings in front. "Those are the rooms for the actors and actresses. Yours are on the top floor. Not underground."

Linlin and I shared a large room. It was clean and well furnished with rugs, couches and antique desks. From the four windows I saw different sides of the mountains, some brown, some green, some yellow, and some purple because of the different plants growing there. And between two mountains I saw the Wu Jiang River.

This is one of the most important rivers in Chinese history, where Xiang Yu, and Shi Dakai, the two famous heroes of peasant uprisings, committed suicide after each failed to overthrow the emperor. Xiang Yu had died two thousand years ago, and Shi Dakai, one hundred years ago.

I decided to go see the river. "Wait," Linlin called after me. "I want to go too. I'd like to wash my handkerchief there."

On the river bank was an old, decrepit wooden temple built in 1855. The columns of the temple were pitted with traces of worm holes. A plaque on one of the weathered columns read: "In Memory of Shi Dakai." It was so worn that I could hardly make out the writing. I touched one of the columns. It felt as if I were touching our history—a history full of wounds and scars. "This is my country," I thought, "with five thousand years of history. This is my country, a country scarred all over with tragic events. One dynasty falls, another rises, but the emperors remain the same."

Linlin was sitting on a big rock in the water, washing a pink handkerchief. "Come, sit by me," she said. A gentle river breeze blew through her long, silken hair, and her lovely figure was silhouetted against the sunset. I thought sadly, "One as beautiful as you should always be surrounded by all that is beautiful in this world."

Our dinner was a grand fish banquet—ten different kinds of fish, all taken just that afternoon from the Wu Jiang River. The five leaders of the mine joined us. They proposed toasts of good health to us all, and I thanked them for receiving Linlin and me into the asbestos mines.

After dinner, the theater director outlined the next day's schedule: from ten o'clock to eleven, practice singing or dancing; lunch at twelve; from twelve to two, nap time; three to four, practice again; at five have a snack, take a shower, then board the bus. The first performance would

174

be at the east mine, thirty minutes away.

I obeyed all the rules except for the noon sleep. Instead, I went out. Following a little rocky road and passing through a basketball court, I came to a shop where people of the Yi nationality were lined up to buy pork. The Yi women wore long, colorful, striped-cotton skirts, with bright square kerchiefs on their heads, and their wooden earrings were big and long. Yi men wore black pants that swept the ground when they walked. Their heads were wrapped in red-striped cloth, with a wild bird's feather inserted at the back. Each wore one feather, long and colorful.

Near the shop was a little restaurant, crowded with Yi. I went in, and bought a roll. It tasted like raw oil and vinegar.

In the late afternoon I was excited because we were going to see the east mine soon. The bus travelled for about thirty minutes, then entered a tunnel guarded by two soldiers. We seemed to be moving further and further down into the earth. After passing by many dazzling lights in the tunnel, we eventually arrived at a wide playground, lit up, and surrounded by tall, red brick flats. "They are the work shops," the theater director told me, and he led Linlin and me into one of them. It was large, with machines installed overhead. The asbestos was piled on the floor, white, shining, and crisp. I picked some up, and it broke into pieces right away in my hand. There were no workers around, and the director explained that all of them had taken the evening off for our performance. "The performance is their only entertainment."

"Why? Are no movies ever shown here?" I asked.

"Yes. But all the movies, plays, and concerts are based on the eight revolutionary operas. The workers are tired of seeing them," he answered.

175

"But to watch the eight revolutionary operas is the revolutionary requirement, isn't it?" I persisted.

"Our workers are not interested in the revolution."

"You mean the Cultural Revolution?"

"That's right. No worker has ever joined it."

"They never stopped producing asbestos during the Cultural Revolution?"

"No. The mine leaders are not interested in politics. They ask only that the workers work hard for the country, and they pay them two or three times more money than before."

"Did the government actually allow this place to escape the Cultural Revolution?"

"This mine enjoys special treatment, the government's Minority Policy called 'For the Freedom of Minority Nationalities to Be Respected.'"

The East Mine Theater was modern. The curtain, stage lights, microphones, everything was new and of excellent quality. I performed first, singing a popular song. The applause proved I was successful. Linlin's ballet, "The White-Haired Girl," was the last act. She was successful, too. Many workers stood up to cheer and took pictures of us.

The next evening, we performed in the west mine. Each day we changed to a new mine. We performed 20 acts in each show. On weekends we were free, and almost every miner's family invited us for dinner. They lived behind the mountains, in flats. Each family seemed quite rich. They had expensive furniture and gave wonderful dinners. Most of them were Yi people. However, I noticed some were very thin, their skin was very yellow, and many were coughing badly. Later on I learned that all these problems were caused by the asbestos dust. I also learned many workers suffered from lung cancer.

Time passed quickly at the mines. Linlin was quite happy. She told me that in one of her dreams she was sitting by our beloved Premier Zhou Enlai on an airplane, eating grapes. She often wrote to her mother and sent money home. Each time I reminded her not to put our exact address on the envelopes and I checked them carefully. I sometimes added a sentence to her letters, asking her mother to visit my parents and tell them that I was with Linlin and everything was fine.

Linlin had learned Yi and Tibetan dances, and I learned many new folk songs. But I sometimes felt empty, especially when I was alone. To try to get rid of the feeling, I forced myself to memorize at least five English words a day, from the little English dictionary. I kept writing my diaries too. But I still felt empty.

"I like this place very much," Linlin told me. "I want to stay here forever, because nobody here knows my family background, and they don't discriminate against me."

Holding Linlin's hands I couldn't say anything. I felt sorry about her past, but at the same time I envied her happiness. I wanted to be happy too, but I couldn't. I needed books. I needed many books. I needed a large library. There was no library here at all and no bookstore.

Linlin made many friends. Some worked in shops, some were soldiers. They came to visit her frequently, and Linlin went to visit them. I didn't make any close friends, although people were kind to me. I felt they didn't understand me. They liked to talk about things that didn't interest me—hair styles, clothes, and fashions. One day I found a picture magazine in the dining hall. I took it home and began to copy its drawings. I drew many people, and I talked with them.

It was October now. We had been at the mine for two months. The fall in the mountains was hot and dry. During weekends, I spent evenings walking along the banks of the Wu Jiang River. I liked to see my footprints left in the sand and to watch the sunset falling on the river. One evening the sunset was unusually beautiful—seven colored rays. With the waves moving, the rays broke into patterns, square, round, ellipse, and triangle. Then all the patterns joined together, forming a house as shining as a crystal palace.

"How do you do?" I heard a man's voice and saw him standing nearby, smiling.

"How do you do?" He spoke again, and I found he was standing beside me. I was a little upset because he had disturbed me.

"What are you searching for in the deep water?" he asked, with humor.

"Nothing."

"But why do you sit here for more than an hour?"

"I enjoy the cool."

"What's your name?

"What's your name?" I retorted.

"My name is Tian Yuan."

"Fields," I said, realizing that the characters for his name were related to farming. "You've got a good name. You must love being a peasant and working in the fields every day. Are you a high school student?"

"Me? I'm too old to be a student. I'm over thirty."

"What are you doing, then?"

"A news reporter for the Chengdu Evening Newspaper."

"You must have reported that to go to the countryside is glorious and a great pleasure," I said.

"Are all news reporters liars?" He gave me a half smile.

"But the newspapers do lie all the time," I replied. "At the beginning of the Cultural Revolution they said that to destroy the Four Olds was Chairman Mao's great strategy. Later they said to destroy the capitalist roaders was Mao's strategy. Then they said that sending all the high school students to the countryside was the strategy. What *is* the strategy? Does it change with the weather?"

"Are you a high school student?"

"Me? I am an ordinary Chinese citizen." Not wanting to talk to him, I looked into the river.

"Do you enjoy writing?"

"Why do you ask me such a strange question?"

"You'll be a good writer." I was surprised. I turned to look at him.

"Could you tell me why you often sit here to study the water?" he continued.

"How do you know?"

"I've watched you here for two weeks now."

"How long have you been here?"

"Three weeks."

"What are you going to report for the newspaper?"

"That's my secret. I won't tell you until you tell your name." I gave it to him.

"I like your name. You must be from a learned family. Did your parents choose that name for a special reason?"

"Don't talk nonsense. Tell me, what are you going to report?"

He frowned a little, then said, "I will report on the wise leadership here who refused to join in the turmoil."

The word "turmoil" startled me. Clearly, he meant the Cultural Revolution. I was moved, and stretched out my hand. He shook it and asked, "Will you do me a favor? Describe the big mountain in front of us?"

"It's a tiger, a big black tiger that opens its bloody mouth," I said.

"Have you ever seen a tiger?"

"Yes. But only in nightmares. The tiger always tried to swallow me."

Tian Yuan looked into my eyes for a while, excited. Then he said, "Would you describe what you have seen in the river?"

"A palace. A quiet, crystal palace. All the doors are closed. At the window I saw angels. Each held an apple, a gold apple. They were dancing beautifully to heavenly music. They were so happy and peaceful. How I wish I could join them, to be one of their guests."

"Wonderful," he exclaimed, and tightly gripped my hands. "Wonderful."

The sunset was now gone. The river had become dark. We began walking home. Tian Yuan invited me to go boating with him the next day.

It was a pleasant Sunday morning. Tian Yuan and a young Yi boy were sitting on a large bamboo-made craft in the river, waiting for me. "His name is Noo Noo." Tian Yuan introduced us. When I held his hand, Noo Noo blushed. He was shy and around eighteen years of age. As Noo Noo paddled, I asked Tian Yuan how he could borrow a craft from a Yi.

He smiled. "I can go into a tiger's mouth if I want to." Then he told me he was familiar with this area and had been to the mines five times. He liked it here very much.

"Why are you so interested in this area?" I asked.

"I'm writing a book. I chose the asbestos mines for the background of my book."

"What's your book about?"

"The Cultural Revolution."

"When are you expecting it to be published?"

"In two hundred years," he laughed. "I write it not because I want to publish it, but because I want to tell the truth."

"Where is the truth?" I mocked.

"The truth seems to be kidnapped and tied up, but it's not dead yet. Remember an ancient poem?—'The wild fire burns the grass this year, but it will grow again next year.'"

"When do you think the truth will be set free?"

"When a new government is born." He looked away.

"Is there any possibility?"

"We'll wait for Deng Xiaoping. He is the only man who can turn China around."

Tian Yuan told me all the Yi people here liked Deng Xiaoping.

We arrived at a narrow, rushing section of the river.

"I like Deng Xiaoping," I said. "He talks sense. Remember his saying, 'No matter if it is a white cat or a black cat, so long as it can catch a rat, it is a good cat'?"

Tian Yuan nodded and told me that all the Yi people here called Deng Xiaoping "Deng Qing Tian," or "Deng of the Clear Skies."

"I wish him a long, long life," I said.

"All the Chinese wish him the same, but ..." he stopped.

"But Mao doesn't like him, right?" I continued his sentence. "Nevertheless, our beloved Premier Zhou wants Deng as his successor. Surely that counts, doesn't it?

Tian Yuan looked very sad. "Premier Zhou has no power in the government anymore. He has been forbidden to act. He doesn't even have the freedom to speak. Now he is very ill, and most of his nurses in the hospital are plainclothes agents sent by Jiang Qing. There is a story about how he once tried to talk with Deng Xiaoping, when Deng visited him in the hospital. As Deng sat down, Zhou asked a nurse

181

for a little apple. Then Zhou placed the apple in front of Deng, took a knife and stabbed it from the side, his eyes fixed on Deng. As you know, "little apple" is a homonym for Deng's name, 'Xiaoping.' Zhou was trying to warn Deng to watch out for those who might stab him in the back.

We both sighed. Tian Yuan went on:

"He has protected many leaders in the central government, and also their families. Our Premier's heart is one with the people. That's why Mao couldn't drive him out of the central government, even by launching the Cultural Revolution."

Yuan asked Noo Noo to row to the bank. He helped me off the craft and up a mountain.

On the other side I saw a little, dusty building at the foot of the mountain. "It's a political jail," Tian Yuan told me. A group of people came out of the building. They were led by policemen. Their heads were shaved and they bowed, silently walking into another mountain. "They are sentenced to life to work in an asbestos mine, where the conditions are very bad. The asbestos dust is as thick as three inches on the ground."

We sat down on a rock, and he told me how he had been held in a political jail in Chengdu for months at the beginning of the Cultural Revolution. "They accused me of trying to erase my father's political spot—he was labeled a rightist in 1957."

I didn't want to hear these things. I didn't want to know that so many innocent people were being persecuted. I thought of all the people I knew who had suffered because of the Cultural Revolution—my friends, my teachers, my father. Some were still in jail.

Walking down to the road I didn't want to talk. We sat down to have lunch, orange juice and bread. "Noo, Noo, would you like to tell this lovely lady about your Torch Festival?" Tian Yuan asked, trying to make me happy.

"It's a night festival for boys and girls," Noo Noo said and blushed. "We dance all night. And make friends. We blow bamboo for music."

After lunch, Noo Noo paddled us home, and on the way Tian Yuan told me more about the Torch Festival.

"It's a once-a-year festival that starts on July 21 and continues to August 7. Boys and girls from this area meet in the woods by blowing short flutes. They play love songs. Each plays a different one. If a boy's song attracts a girl, she will immediately sing to him in the same melody. Then they meet. They talk to each other, dance together, and when it gets dark, they go to a secluded place to make love. They are free to have sex. But pregnancy is taboo." This aroused my curiosity and I asked:

"Do they know something about birth control?"

"They have their own abortion methods. Very primitive."

"Abortion?"

"Yes. If the abortion methods don't work, pregnant girls must kill themselves."

"That's so cruel."

"That's their custom."

"Why don't the pregnant ones get married instead of committing suicide? Do you know about Yi marriage?"

"Well, the wedding ceremony is serious. It's exactly the same with the funeral ceremony: first, horse racing, then banqueting. All the Yi in the area must attend the ceremony, even new-born babies. The banquet is composed of roast pigs—whole pigs with the bristles still on them. But as soon as the wedding ceremony is over, the bride goes home to live with her own parents, and continues to join in the torch festival until she gets pregnant, by a man at the festival. Then she starts sleeping with her husband, and stops going to the torch festival."

"You mean the first child of a Yi couple is never the husband's?"

"Right, that's the Yi custom."

"Who takes care of the child?"

"The husband."

"But he is not the real father."

"But he takes care of the child. That's the Yi's custom."

"Can Yi girls find husbands in the torch festival?"

"No. Girls are not allowed to ask the boys' names."

"Then how does a Yi girl find a husband?"

"Through her parents and a go-between. The groom must pay a large amount of money to the bride's parents and the go-between before the wedding."

"How do Yi boys get money?"

"They hunt, and dig herbs in these mountains. The government buys animal skins and herbs from them."

Tian Yuan soon left our mines. The night before he left for Chengdu, we sat at the edge of the Wu Jiang River and had a long conversation. I asked him why all the people in China could have been fooled by one person in the Cultural Revolution, and he said, "China missed one important historical period—capitalism. Our history had been artificially pushed into a leap from feudalism to communism. That's why people had no idea about democracy and freedom. They believed in Mao the way they had believed in an emperor, and they completely obeyed." This point was reasonable to me, and I could see how Mao could launch such a movement because he knew he was an emperor in so many people's minds, and he took advantage of this. But he was too cruel. He let thousands and thousands of people die for him, to serve his purpose of getting rid of Liu Shaoqi. Did Mao ever think that things would reverse if they were pushed to the extreme? Did he never suspect that he was using his own hands to bury himself deep in China's hatred? Mao, the cruelest feudal emperor in China will be judged sooner or later by history itself. Meanwhile, he has left China with a most humiliating memory.

Then, Tian Yuan told me a great story about Kao Yi, a famous novelist in Sichuan.

"His home was ransacked thirty times by Red Guards. They took away all his books and paper. But in a struggle meeting before thousands of people, Kao Yi bowed his head, not out of fear but because he was thinking up another novel."

That was a delightful night. The waves of the Wu Jiang River rippled with the lights from the mines on the mountains, and, from a distance, I heard the melody of a Yi love song.

"Were you ever in love?" Tian Yuan asked.

"No," I didn't want to talk about Deng He.

"Do you think you'll love someone some day?"

"Never."

"I respect you," he said. "But please write to me. I am your friend, and if I can help you in any way, please let me know."

Winter came. The air in the mines became very dry. Every day Linlin and I had to put drops of oil into our noses so they would not bleed.

Noo Noo often came to visit me. He brought me a lot of tonic herbs, and told me to eat them immediately. He said I was too thin. One day he brought me the gall bladder of a bear, telling me it was the best tonic. The bear had been hunted down by his father years ago. He told me Yi people living in the far mountains didn't go to bed to sleep, but sat on the floor all night. He also told me Yi women loved to carry yellow umbrellas for good luck when visiting friends.

It was the end of March, 1970. We had been at the asbestos mines for half a year. The five leaders of the mines one day asked Linlin and me to a meeting. They told us gravely that the central government had issued a new policy: "Every mine worker's child must go to the countryside immediately. The government is sending to check that this is done."

We had to leave the asbestos mines early next morning. It was so hurried that I didn't get a chance to see Noo Noo. That evening I took my last walk along the Wu Jiang River. I wrapped up a handful of sand in my handkerchief, wanting to keep it forever. "Goodbye, Wu Jiang River, goodbye, asbestos mines. Goodbye, Noo Noo."

Fetching water from the only well in the village.

CHAPTER 16

Settling in the Countryside

林吃扇户

My parents didn't blame me for staying away for half a year. I showed them the bear gall bladder and a big package of insect grass, ginseng and gastrodia elata Noo Noo had given me. I insisted my mother accept the hundred yuan that I had saved in the asbestos mines.

"How is everything at home?" I asked.

"They came to threaten us many times," my mother said. "We showed them the note you wrote telling that you had run away. They finally gave up." But, she said, the Party Secretary in her company was kind. He promised to employ me as a clerk in his office, if I agreed to go to the countryside first.

I didn't believe it.

"He is a good man," my mother said. "He never cheats people."

"I don't know him, and I don't believe him. I don't

believe anyone who tells me to go to the countryside."

"But I know he is a good person. That's why I loaned him two hundred yuan last year when his father died. At that time nobody dared lend him money because he was called a capitalist roader."

"You mean now he is no longer a capitalist roader? So he asks me to go to the countryside?"

"There is no capitalist roader, especially since the Cultural Revolution is over."

"Who said the revolution is over? I haven't gone to the countryside yet." I laughed.

"But in fact it is over. First, Chairman Liu has been overthrown. Second, the high school students have been driven out to the countryside. Third, the counter-revolutionaries have been put into jails."

"Counterrevolutionaries?"

"Yes. Those who supported the rebel Red Guards in the revolution are now called counterrevolutionaries. They have now been jailed. Five young men in my company, and eleven in your father's company were arrested, and many of your teachers were arrested."

"Hell! I don't believe anyone is a counterrevolutionary. People supported the rebel Red Guards because they listened to Mao!"

"All right. Let's not talk about the revolution anymore," father put in.

That night I thought much about my future, and I saw clearly I would have to go to the countryside. It was the only way. I didn't want to bring my parents any more trouble and I didn't want them to have to support me again. They seemed to have aged a lot since I last saw them. They must have suffered much because of me during my half-year's absence.

190

I was nearly twenty-two years old, an adult. I tried to comfort myself with the thought that four out of every five Chinese are peasants who live in the countryside generation after generation. Why not me? "Go!" I said to myself. "You will survive!"

I went to see Linlin. Her mother took me aside and asked me to have her daughter with me in the same village.

"When Linlin is with you I feel at ease," she said.

I decided to try and have Linlin accepted to the same commune my school had months before arranged for me. It was called the Sunflower Commune. We planned to stay at home one more week to prepare.

One afternoon I went to the City No. 1 Department Store to buy a quilt. At the entrance I saw Teacher Wei, the math instructor who had invited the Beijing Red Guard to give lectures in his apartment.

"How are you?" He greeted me in a hardly audible voice. "Let's go to the park." His expression told me he had something important to say.

After a five-minute walk in silence, we entered the park. We went to the end where there was a lake and we sat down on a rock surrounded by bushes; no other people were around. I looked at Teacher Wei, expecting him to tell me something important, but he just looked at me quietly, with a serene smile.

"How are you doing these days?" I asked. He just smiled. "Do you enjoy the lake here?"

He nodded without a word. "I am going to the countryside in a few days," I said.

He didn't respond.

I was disappointed at his silence and I wondered why he had invited me here if he had nothing to say. Each time I looked at him, he returned to me his serene smile. He doesn't really want to talk to me, after all, I thought, and decided to relax. I gazed into the lake, absentmindedly wondering if there were still fish in it. An hour passed, and it looked like it might rain soon, so I stood up and said good-bye.

That evening I kept wondering why Teacher Wei hadn't said a word to me. The next morning, the local radio station announced Wei had committed suicide in a reform camp. He used a razor to cut the artery in his leg under the quilt at night. He was found dead in a pool of blood hours later.

The newspaper indicated that he had refused to confess though he had been interrogated for three months; that, before the suicide, he had run away for a whole afternoon.

Holding the newspaper, my hands were shaking. I didn't know Teacher Wei had been jailed. I would never have imagined that he would risk death for a few last hours of freedom. And in one of those hours he had chosen to be with me. I felt so bad, so guilty. I should have tried to help him in some way. I should have at least asked him if he was in some sort of difficulty. I should have stayed longer with him that afternoon . . .

There would be no funeral ceremony for him, the newspaper continued, because he was a "counterrevolutionary who had hidden a Beijing rebel Red guard in his apartment and given him the chance to spread his reactionary ideas to the people."

I let the newspaper drop from my hands. Teacher Wei was dead. Our wonderful teacher. He had always been so good to us students. Now he was dead. His ashes were in a box and would be buried, no one knew where. Teacher Wei, why didn't you say something to me before you went away? Why? . . .

Linlin and I took a bus, a train and a boat. Finally we

arrived at the Sunflower Commune. As I reported my name to the commune officer, the Party Secretary came out. He stuck up his thumb and exclaimed, "You are the sweetest part of sugar cane. Good girl! We have read your school file. You are the best student in your school. And we have been waiting for you for almost one year. Where have you been?"

I smiled politely and introduced Linlin to him. "Sir, could you arrange for Linlin to be in the same village with me?"

"We haven't read her file and don't know her family background. We can't arrange for her to be in your village because it is an advanced village."

"What do you mean? My friend Linlin is a wonderful student. She is at the top in her class." Linlin lowered her head.

After some hesitation the Party Secretary said, "All right, we'll arrange for her to go to the number two team village which is close to yours."

"What is my village?" I asked.

"The number five team village. The Brigade Party Secretary and the Brigade Chairman both live there."

Two peasant men guided us to the different villages. It was afternoon. As we passed the fields, all the villagers stopped to watch us. "These two girls are different from the other students. They wear beautiful clothes. They must come from the big city, Chengdu," a man said.

"Beautiful? Take one home as your woman," another peasant joked with him. They all laughed loudly.

After crossing two hills, Linlin and I separated. When I arrived in my village it was almost dark. The village houses were made of brick, and built around courtyard compounds. The village gate was of stone. Through the gate I could see the villagers standing crowded together in a large yard. The yard floor was paved with cement. Many dogs were barking.

"Welcome," a middle-aged woman greeted me and came to carry my baggage to the house in which I would be living. "Call me Zhong Fong," she said. "I'm the team leader for women peasants here."

The house was behind the village gate. It was very large and dark inside. Zhong Fong struck a match and I could see the room had no window. There was a bare double bed, a long black wooden bench, and a small desk.

As Zhong Fong left, a group of little children crowded into my room. Their faces were spattered with mud and none had shoes. I asked them to tell me where I could get water to clean the dusty furniture, and they showed me a pond near the house.

They watched as I scrubbed and finally a little boy asked, "Like it here?"

"Me?" I answered. "Yes, because I have so many little friends in my house."

"But the three girls didn't like it here," another boy said.

"They lived in this house?"I asked.

"Yes, but they've moved. They saw a ghost in this house." "A ghost?"

"Yes . . . an old man's ghost. He hanged himself here," a girl said.

"Nonsense. I don't believe in ghosts. If I saw that ghost right now, I would ask him to help me clean this house."

"He comes out at midnight. Then he shakes the bed and tells you to leave the bed for him," a little girl added.

"Listen," I said, "if any of you want to be my friends you have to stop talking about ghosts. Do you want to be my friends?"

"Yes!" they all cheered in chorus.

It was dark now, and all the children went home. I opened my bedding and found two packages and a purse. One contained a bottle of honey and the other lard, which I guessed must be from my mother. The purse contained one hundred yuan.

Zhong Fong came in again with a basket in her right hand. "These are your provisions," she said, and showed me to my kitchen.

It was across the yard, a small straw room, the only place made of straw. "Why is the kitchen made of straw?" I asked. "It could catch on fire so easily."

"You're too demanding. Seems a big brick house to sleep in is not enough. Now you demand a brick kitchen. What'll you want next?" Zhong Fong answered.

I was stunned. I didn't expect such hostility.

"Here are your matches." She handed me a little match box. "Remember, there's a shortage of matches so don't waste them." She struck a match to light a lamp made from an empty ink bottle. It was standing on a low table in the corner. Then she left.

I was hungry, but the mud stoves in the center of the kitchen worried me. There were two, connected to each other, both as tall as I was. Between the two stoves was a channel, which was designed to carry fire from one to the other. On one stove there was an iron wok, as big as my two arms stretched apart. Overhead there was a cover made of baked clay, suspended on a cord from the kitchen roof.

Dry straw and wheat stalks, piled high behind the kitchen door, were the fuel for the fire. There was a rusted iron bucket half full of water. The table was as short as a little chair and contained two drawers. I opened them: inside were a pair of chopsticks, a rough rice bowl, a spatula, a bamboo brush, and a little pot of salt.

I carried two bowlfuls of water to the wok and washed it with the bamboo brush. I put four handfuls of rice into the wok and covered it with twice as much water. I moved the low table to the stove, stood on it, trying to reach the clay cover. But it was too high and I gave up.

I started the fire, but most of the heat escaped to the other stove, because it was open with no wok on it. I cooked my rice for an hour, and I used up half my fuel. At last it smelled like food. I grabbed the spatula to scoop up the rice into my bowl, but discovered that half of the rice had turned into burnt crust sticking to the bottom of the wok.

I was hungry. I put some salt on the rice and began to eat. The burnt rice was too hard to chew, so I put some lard on it. The rice then became a little softer and tasted good.

The village was asleep; every house was dark. I brought the little table out to the yard, and sat there to eat. Two dogs came out; they were chasing each other. The moon was rising over the mountain in front of me, curved and yellow in the deep blue sky. This reminded me of Deng He, of the night we met at the boat. I hurried back into the house and closed the door.

Early next morning Zhong Fong kicked loudly at my door to wake me up. She shouted, "Out! To the fields! You should know you came to the countryside to receive your education from us peasants, not to sleep like a pig. Chairman Mao teaches us, 'All the high school students must eat like a peasant, sleep like a peasant, and work in the field like a peasant.'"

I got up. This woman was really something, I thought. She even used Mao's quotation to wake me up in the early morning.

I opened the door, and she handed me a big rusty hoe. "Go to the fields with me," she ordered, although she knew I had had no breakfast.

The hoe was so big and heavy that it took both my arms

to lift it to my shoulders. To try to be friendly with her, I said, "Leader Zhong, you must teach me how to use this hoe. From now on I am your student, and you are my teacher."

She didn't answer, but just stared at me with a strange expression on her face. After I repeated my words, she said, "You're a bookworm, aren't you? Every word from you is sour. That's why our great leader Chairman Mao orders you, all the stinking bookworms, to come to the country-side to receive education. You don't know how to grow yams, do you? We peasants eat them half the year. You don't know how to grow rice, do you? You know nothing. You know only sour words from the stinking books, capi-talist books."

She was like a gun ready to fire at me, I thought, and decided to say nothing more to her.

The field was on the top of a mountain where about forty women were digging. Some were old, others middle-aged and young. They were talking about something, and laughing loudly. I heard a word, "carrot." But they stopped when they saw me.

I began to dig.

"Have you ever seen a peasant working?" An old lady asked with a kind smile. "We peasants work in the field all year round. We carry the sun on our backs over moun-tains."

I was a bit surprised to hear such a beautiful expression. Another woman joined in, "We bring the moon home every night."

I didn't know how to use a hoe. I couldn't lift it high enough, so when it dropped down it only touched the sur-face of the field. I tried hard, and I held the hoe as tight as I could. Soon both my hands were blistered. I spit on my hands and threw the hoe higher, but it still didn't work. I sweated a lot and I felt hungry.

About twelve, Zhong Fong shrieked "Ooo-Hoo!" At that, all the women threw down their hoes and ran home. "Ooo-Hoo" apparently meant "take a break."

I ran directly to my kitchen, warmed the leftovers and swallowed them. Then Zhong Fong shouted "Ooo-Hoo" again, which meant to start working again, and I ran out to the mountain.

The afternoon job was to gather peas growing on the slope of the mountain. They were very ripe. The vines and leaves were yellow and dry.

"Each person works two rows at a time," Zhong Fong ordered, and all the women began to crouch at the ends of the rows. In that position they moved along up to the mountain top, while they uprooted the peas. Their right hands dealt with the peas on the right side and their left hands with the peas on the left. They moved quickly, as if their bent legs were running. It was amazing. I was soon left far behind.

The women moved up to the end of their rows, and then slid down. Their hands worked as fast as machines. Before I had finished my first two rows, they had started on their fourth pair.

Evening came. Zhong Fong made her very long "Ooo-Hoo" sound and all the women got up and ran down the mountain to the yard.

Sitting in the yard on the ground, I found every one of them wearing a serious face. "What's the matter?" I asked one old woman.

"Evaluation points."

"What's that?"

"Every day we get points from the field work. The highest is eight and the lowest is four. That's money."

"Money? Someone brings you money?"

"Yes. The team leader will give us money twice a year, according to our points."

"How much money for one point?"

"About twenty-three fen. Our village is an advanced village, so we earn more. We earn more money than in a backward village. In a backward village one point earns only eight or ten fen."

"Could they live on that little money?"

"Well, first we don't pay for our houses. And we can borrow food from the commune."

"But how do you pay back the money to the commune?"

"Why do you worry so much? The skies don't fall. The government takes care of everything. Some villagers will pay the money when their kids grow up."

"How many points does a man get a day?"

"The highest is ten, and the lowest is five."

The atmosphere in the yard was tense. Everyone wanted to gain higher points. I decided it would be better if I evaluated my points as the lowest. When my turn came around, I stood up, and said, "I came to the countryside to receive re-education from all of you. But since I am not familiar with field work, and I did a bad job today, I evaluate my points as four." Nobody spoke. After a while Zhong Fong said to the village accountant, who held a thick account book in his hand, "Write it down. She got four points today."

The villagers didn't stand up, and they didn't offer to take low points. Zhong Fong evaluated them one by one. Most of them got seven. Three got eight, and the five young students got four.

As I entered my house I was starving. But the thought

of cooking upset me because my fuel was going to be gone soon. I also worried about the water in the rusty bucket.

After thinking for a while, I decided to go to a neighbor and borrow a pair of clean wooden buckets to fetch fresh water. "Hello, Aunt," I said, "would you lend me your water buckets? In return I will fetch a bucket of water for you." She agreed, and showed me the village well.

I was terribly shocked to see that the well was right beside a cow dung pond. The water ran directly from the cow dung. But it was the only well in the village, and that was the water I had to use to cook. My supper was the same as the night before, rice with salt and lard.

The next morning I was woken up early by the bite of bed bugs. I tried to stand up, but my legs felt soft and sore. They seemed too weak to support me. I tried to move them, but they just crumpled. I struggled to the door, but fell as I opened it.

Two men helped me to my bed. One of them offered to call Linlin. She cried when she saw me. She said she had never believed I would be sick in bed.

"Linlin, I'm okay. Don't be a little girl. You know, yesterday I performed just like a duck, running a little bit too much around the mountains. That's all." Linlin smiled and began to cook for me.

"Where are your eggs and fresh vegetables?" she asked.

"I don't have any."

"Why? You are in an advanced village. Why do the advanced people treat you this way? How can you live without vegetables?"

"Linlin, remember, we are here to receive re-education."

"But I have eggs and vegetables. The villagers gave them to me the night I arrived and they also brought me corn cakes and sugar. I hate your advanced village. I hate the villagers in your village."

"Linlin, don't think of people this way. Many of them are good, and this morning they helped me to my bed and they got you here, didn't they?"

Linlin took care of me for three days. She did not live far, and she knew a short cut to my village that took her only ten minutes.

The fourth day I recovered and I asked Zhong Fong to give me some firewood. But she said, "It's limited. This village is short of firewood."

"Shall I buy some?" I asked.

"Nobody wants your stinking money. You, all of you from the city, stink! You are stinking capitalists." Then she pointed to the mountain behind the house, and said, "Go there to pick up sticks. But don't be greedy. The sticks in that mountain belong to five families."

A week slowly passed. Because of the food, I suffered from constipation. I bled, and it hurt badly.

CHAPTER 17

I Become a Barefoot Doctor

芥 脚医生

One morning, Old Kong, the village pig feeder came to ask me to lend him some money. "I'll return it tomorrow," he assured me. "I need five yuan to buy some vegetable seeds in the market."

"A market? Where is it?" I asked.

"You can get there on foot. Takes thirty minutes. Every five days there is a market. Peasants are free on that day to buy things."

"Can you buy fresh vegetables there?"

"Yes, but you don't have to buy them. You can grow them by yourself. On your free land."

"Where is free land."

"Ask Zhong Fong, She'll give it to you. But you have to ask."

"She doesn't seem to like me."

"Because you didn't give her gifts. She wants gifts."

"What kind of gifts?"

"Anything from the city—clothes, soap, socks, a hat, a scarf, things like that."

"I don't have such things. My clothes are too small for her anyway."

"It doesn't matter. She can give them to her relatives."

I followed Old Kong to the market. There I bought a basket of eggs and many different kinds of fresh vegetables. As I was preparing supper that evening Jiang Shui, the Brigade Party Secretary, appeared at my kitchen door. It was the first time he had come to my kitchen, although we had seen each other every day. He entered and came close to the wok, saying, "Good, you eat well. You eat fried eggs."

Then he said, "Little Comrade, I heard from the commune that you are a member of the Young Communist League. You are one of the advanced people. In our brigade, we hold advanced people meetings every Monday in number seven team village. I think you should join them, and I hope you can join the Communist Party some day. Of course, it takes time to test your political awareness. But I believe you'll be qualified."

"The next morning, as we worked in a cornfield fertilizing the land, Mr. Jiang's daughter said to me, "Do you know Gui Gui, the young man? He's going to be accepted into the Communist Party soon. My father recommended him. You know, my father also recommended him to be the Vice Party Secretary of the brigade. He is very thoughtful. You know, each time he comes to see my father, he brings us a full basket of salted eggs. My father also arranged for his father to work in the brigade co-op, selling sugar and oil, so he doesn't work in the field anymore, suffering in the hot sun."

That evening Jiang's daughter asked me to allow her to

sleep in my house. "My father says your house is big. He told me I could share it with you."

"But there is only one bed," I objected.

"Your bed is a double one. It's wide enough for two people."

I was not used to sleeping with a stranger, and I had begun to detest her father, a brigade leader, fishing for bribes. I decided to move into Linlin's house.

Linlin's village had no brick house and the straw houses were scattered and very shabby. She lived in a narrow, small room, with a window that was no more than a three-inch hole. There was a bed and a table that had already made the room tight. She had no kitchen, but only a little mud stove in the corner outside the door. To protect against rain, a peasant hand made an addition out of that little area by covering it with plastic. The right side of Linlin's room was the wall of a cow shed where eight cows from the village were kept. After supper I went for a walk, but as soon as I opened the door, I was completely surrounded by a dense cloud of mosquitos. I retreated, and Linlin told me the mosquitoes were bigger than normal because they feasted on the cows. Their bites stung like fire. At night the cows snored like thunder.

The next morning, when I returned to my village for work, Zhong Fong accosted me. "You have no right to live in another village. You came here to receive re-education from our village. You must receive it completely. You must eat in our village, sleep in our village, and labor in our village. The village is your school. If you are not honest in staying here, we will never give you a political diploma. You know what that means."

I moved back. Jiang's daughter no longer tried to move in with me.

204

I asked my father to send me a gas stove, and from then on I cooked my food in my bedroom, with the door shut.

I worked hard in the fields and tried to have as little conversation as possible with Zhong Fong and Jiang's daughter. In three months I gradually learned how to manage the hard field work, and I earned eight points a day. In cutting wheat, a job regarded as the hardest in the field, I even left many women behind me.

Life seemed somewhat normal, and I resumed my English studies in the evening. But often in the evenings the villagers would come to my house for a chat. Sometimes they stayed the whole evening. From these chats I learned that most of them suffered from rheumatism since they often complained about bad backs and bad legs. I wanted to help them. I wrote to father asking him to buy me acupuncture needles and medical books. I studied the books and tried the needles on my own body to make sure I was doing it right. Little by little I started treating the villagers. The acupuncture worked fantastically. It cured almost everyone's ailments. I was very happy.

From one of the books, I learned that a burnt needle would be more effective, so I tried that new method on my knee. It felt good. Seeing me using the new way on my own body, an old man asked me to try it on his bad knee. He had suffered from rheumatism for three years. I tried it on him once, and the next morning he came to tell me his knee was much better.

One afternoon, a little child fell into a ditch, and his forehead bled badly. I carried the child down the mountain to my house, cleaned the wound with boiled water and put musk on it, which Noo Noo had given me. The musk immediately stopped his bleeding. The next day the child was able to walk all the way to my house to show me the success of the treatment.

The villagers began to call me a "barefoot doctor"—a term from Mao's 6:26 Medical Document issued in the Cultural Revolution, in which Mao called upon all the medical workers, doctors, researchers and nurses to leave their hospitals in the cities and go to the mountain villages to bring treatment to the peasants. In a way, I was a barefoot doctor. Like the barefoot doctors throughout the country, I mainly worked in the fields and did medical work in my spare time unless there was an emergency. Because they are peasants and often work barefoot, especially in the south in the paddy fields, they became known as barefoot doctors. But I didn't feel qualified—the rural barefoot doctors had usually been sent to medical courses by their communes. I had only my books, but I continued because it was working.

Many patients, even from other villages came to see me. One day a couple carried their little girl to me and asked me to fix the child's broken arm. A woman insisted that I deliver her first baby. I was, of course, not skilled enough to handle such cases, so I gave them money and urged them to go to the city to see a professional doctor.

With all these new activities I found little time to study my English. I forced myself to learn at least two English words a day, but many evenings, as soon as I opened the English dictionary, I fell asleep.

Now the villagers accepted me as one of them, and shared their jokes with me. In the fields they talked a great deal about sex. If someone's husband was away, they joked to her, "Well, how do you feel these days without a carrot?" And if someone was pregnant, they would ask, "How many times did it take to make the baby?" or "Did you make your baby in the dark or in the lamplight?" They also liked to talk about how the empresses in olden times chose their male concubines. "Do you know how the Tang Empress Wu Ze Tian chose hers?" one woman asked, and then continued, "She didn't care about talent or a handsome face. She just wanted that one thing, the carrot big, long and strong. She lined up the men naked in her imperial chamber. Once she found the man she wanted she would grab his carrot and slobber 'Oh, so marvelous!'" We all laughed.

The men's jokes were also funny. They made fun of Mao's quotations by changing some of the words. One quotation was: "Don't always think of yourself but always think of other people." They changed the words "think of" to "fuck up," and laughed loudly.

The village had no theater. A movie was shown once every other month in a commune eight miles away. If you went to see the movie you had to bring your own stool along. I went once with the villagers. That night, walking back in the pitch dark for hours, I was so tired I felt as if I could fall asleep right along the road.

Linlin didn't come to visit me often because she hated the leaders of my village. We usually met in the market. Her village advanced her seven yuan a month, allowing her to return it at the end of the year when her work points were checked out. My father sent me eight yuan a month, which was enough for me. In the market Linlin showed me how to buy good things at low prices. She was an expert at finding bargains.

We met many other students at the market. They came from other cities, and some had been in the countryside for nearly two years. Xiao Wang, who played the violin well, told us of a shocking incident that happened near this area a year earlier. He said twenty students had come to

Chu Qi village to visit their friends. They felt sad when talking about the future—and angry, because they were all talented high school graduates who should have had a chance to obtain a college education. They drank, and got drunk. Then they went to the commune restaurant to demand a free meal. After eating, they took everything valuable away from the restaurant. That evening they decided to hold a "Hundred-Chicken Banquet" in which all the dishes were made with chicken. So they went to steal chickens from the peasants, and, after the big meal, they fell soundly asleep. But at midnight their houses were surrounded by peasants armed with pickaxes and sickles. The peasants broke down the doors and killed every one of the students there. Some students tried to escape from the house but because it was night they got lost in the fields. The peasants had torches, found the students, and hacked them to death.

This mass murder enraged all the students in the area. Many returned to the cities and wrote petitions to the central government. Half a month later the central government issued a "Document Concerning the Educated Youth." It stated that anyone, no matter from what commune, area, or team, who is caught bullying or persecuting an educated youth, would be punished according to law. After this document, peasants or officials of the communes who had raped girl students were sent to jail. Those who harassed girls were also sent to jail. I heard a tale of a brigade leader knocking on the door of a girl student one night, saying, "I want to borrow your hen." (which in local dialect meant he wanted to have sex with her), and he was also sent to jail. Yet the incident in which many peasants killed so many students was never pursued. It was said that the incident was the result of a spontaneous action of peasants furious at their property being stolen. It was not organized, not planned and not controlled from behind by counter-revolutionaries. So that was that. The families of the dead were not even compensated in any way. One of the murdered, I learned, was Huang Ming, a handsome, lovable young man of twenty from my school. He was an only son. The mother was so grief-stricken she could not bear to come and claim her son's body.

Winter came. It was cold. My parents sent me a new quilt. Even with this I often didn't sleep well at night. The house couldn't keep out the mountain winds. In winter our field job was to plow the rice pond. This was done by walking barefoot in the rice pond, using our feet to mix the pond water with mud. The severe cold of the water pierced through my bones. There were also many leeches in the water, which could puncture through the flesh of a person's legs right into the muscles. It was horrible. An old man told me to smack my legs before the leeches could make their holes, and he also told me to put vegetable oil on my legs to keep the leeches away. I didn't have much vegetable oil because it was rationed. So I put gasoline on my legs, which seemed to work.

My menstrual periods became irregular because of the barefoot work in the icy pond. Sometimes they never came, and many times they lasted for over twenty days. I grew thin and weak, and my heart beat very fast, as if it were about to leap out of me.

One day Sparrow, a former classmate, came to see me. He told me he was going to become a factory worker.

"How come?" I asked.

"Because I burned down my house."

"You burned down your house?"

"Yes, you know, I lived on an isolated mountain. My house was far away from any of the villagers. It was on the top of the mountain. I put a match to it one night. When the house was almost gone, I ran to report the fire to the village leader. I told him it was an accident. By then, of course, it was too late to save it."

"What did he do then?"

"He said the village didn't have money to build a new house for me. So I mentioned that I would like to go to Xinjiang on the border with the Soviet Union."

"You wanted to flee to the Soviet Union?"

"No. I wanted to go to find a job on a farm there. It is said that a farm in Xinjiang pays well. I borrowed money and bought my ticket. I got to Urumqi, the provincial capital. But I was free to go about for only a week, before the police took me into custody because my clothes were different and my dialect was different. I was detained in Xinjiang for a another week, that's all. Then they sent me back to my mountain village."

"Why did they detain you?"

"They said no student is allowed to look for a job on a state farm. Everyone must follow Mao's call, and receive re-education in a poor mountain village, arranged by his school.

"What happened then?"

"The village leader recommended me to the Air Clarify Factory because that factory just came to my village to find an employee."

"You are lucky," I shook his hand. "Congratulations! Tell me when are you starting you new job?"

"The day after tomorrow."

"Do you think many factories are going to hire students from the countryside?"

"I think so."

On September 13, 1971, a plane carrying Lin Biao and his family was shot down near the border of Mongolia.

The official report was that Lin had been trying to defect to the Soviet Union and his plane was shot down on the order of Premier Zhou Enlai. Mao's successor had turned out to be a national traitor. The news shook me, but somehow it also gave me a new hope for our country.

My health grew worse and worse. I lost weight daily. Linlin urged me to go to see a doctor. She was very worried. I finally decided to go to Chengdu, to my Old Aunt.

Old Aunt found me a good traditional doctor. He said my body had lost Yin-Yang balance. He gave me a prescription called "Relaxation," an herbal brew that he told me to drink twice a day.

I saw my cousin, Brother Yong, again. He looked strong and happy. His face was bright. "Brother Yong, you must have met with good luck. You look wonderful, as if you are twenty years younger," I joked.

He smiled. Then he said seriously: "Now I've finally come to understand the great significance of the Cultural Revolution. The revolution is very necessary for China. The revolutionary situation in my school is excellent."

"Excellent? You must have gotten a wonderful job!"

"Yes. I got a job as a news reporter for the Liberation Daily, the Chengdu army newspaper. But to help solve the problems left over from the revolution, I'll have to remain at Sichuan University for some time."

"Congratulations on becoming a big political liar," I said.

"Don't talk like that. Be serious. I don't like anyone joking about politics."

"Brother Yong, I'm glad that you've changed into a serious person. You know, I've changed too. I've changed into a peasant. Every morning I carry the sun on my back over mountains and every evening I bring the moon home. Isn't that poetic? As Comrade Mao Zedong says, to go to the countryside is a great joy."

"Don't talk like that. You are twenty-two years old. You are a big woman now. You must be mature."

"Thank you for being such a big mature man. Would you like to report on the glorious countryside life? Will you report about the leeches in the rice pond? Report that the village well connects with a cow dung pond? Would you also like to report about me being sick?"

"You are not sick. You are just a little tired. Relax for two days and you will be well. Listen, I'd like to take you to my school. You'd like that, wouldn't you?"

I was sorry to see Sichuan University's gate now guarded by two armed soldiers. We went in. Stopping at a red building, Yong pointed to a big lecture room and announced, "This is my office."

"How did you become such a big official as to have such a big office?"

He didn't answer.

In the room I saw twelve students, including Fang Mei, one of Yong's roommates I had met on my last visit. I smiled at him, but he didn't respond. He just lowered his head. The others lowered their heads, too. They all looked pale.

"What are they doing here?" I asked Yong in a low voice.

"They are criminals. All of them are 8.26 members."

"Who said the 8.26 members are criminals?"

"They used guns. They killed people in the Cultural Revolution."

"But many people used guns in the revolution. Chairman Mao told them to."

"Chairman Mao never told anybody to use guns."

I didn't want to talk to Brother Yong any more. He

didn't respect facts. Remembering the time when a woman in the school slapped him in public and called him a pumpkin seed, I couldn't help laughing. Why didn't he draw a lesson from the Cultural Revolution?

"What are you laughing about?" he asked.

"Nothing." But my thoughts were of a decayed log. Who would be able to carve anything on it?

I sat down and heard Yong shouting at the "criminals," "Confess! You must confess your crime. I give each of you two more days."

The "criminals" were silent. They lowered their heads.

"Fang Mei, come show your confession," Yong shouted.

Fang came over.

"How many people have you killed during the Cultural Revolution?" Yong asked.

"None. I didn't kill anyone," he replied in a flat matter-of-fact tone.

"Yes, you did! I have all the information here. You must correct your political attitude."

"I didn't kill anybody."

To try to deal with Fang Mei individually, because Fang was tough, Brother Yong took the other "criminals" to another room. As soon as Brother Yong walked out the door, I said quickly to Fang, "I want to help you. Do you need me to send letters out?"

"Yes, thank you. Tomorrow?"

Yong returned. He yelled some more at Fang. I pretended to read a newspaper.

At noon Brother Yong went out to buy tomatoes, which he knew I liked best with noodles. I then took the chance to ask Fang "What happened to the other 8.26 members?"

"They got bad jobs. They were assigned to be elementary teachers in Xi Chang District, an area of leprosy. Before

213

they went they were made to feed cows in Shi Fang Farm for three months."

"How long do you think you will be under house arrest here?"

"Maybe the rest of my life." He looked very sad.

The next day I returned with Yong. I carried my schoolbag. Fang looked nervous. I pretended to read a newspaper. As soon as Yong went out, I opened my bag, and Fang quickly threw in his letters.

After lunch, I said goodbye to Yong, and took the bus back to my aunt's house. Fang had written three letters on the confession sheet he had been given. There was no envelope. One letter was for me:

> Dear friend,
>   I don't know how to thank you. You are the only person to give me your smile here. I will always remember you in my heart. Thank you again and again.
>   Fang Mei

The second letter was to his girl friend. It was a sad letter. He said he missed her every day, and that he might never see her again. The letter was beautifully written and very emotional. It expressed deep feeling. The third was to his brother. I put the letters in envelopes, addressed them, and mailed them that afternoon.

Two weeks later, my health was much better, and I returned to my village.

To avoid the sun's heat we cut wheat at night.

CHAPTER 18

Fate

I went to see Linlin. I brought her an album and a pretty pen. Linlin told me the Party Secretary of my mother's company had been there three days before and that some factory workers had come to the commune to hire good students.

"Do they come to hire students like Sparrow, who burned down his house?" I joked.

Linlin was worried. She said she was afraid no factory would hire her because of her family background.

"Linlin," I promised her, "if my mother's leader wants to hire me, I will ask him to hire both of us. If he only needs one, I will let you go. Believe me, Linlin."

A week passed, and I didn't hear anything about employment. But three weeks later my mother wrote me that her company had hired a peasant's child instead of a city student.

Many factories came to our commune to hire city students. But they hired only those who were highly recommended by the village leaders, Brigade leaders and commune leaders. I began to be concerned over our situation. How could we possibly get so many recommendations from so many of them? There were too many to take care of. And why would they recommend Linlin and me, since we had never bribed them?

However, one day Linlin was hired by the Chengdu Steel Factory.

"That's wonderful, Linlin!" I was very happy for her.

But Linlin was depressed. "The worker who hired me asked me to marry him."

"Really? What did you say to him?"

"I agreed."

"Are you sure you want to marry him?"

"I don't know. But otherwise I would never get a chance to go back to a city."

Two days later I saw Linlin off. She just cried.

My field job now was to cut side growths off cotton plants. The plants were about twenty inches high. We had to do the job in the early morning. The dew on the plants wet my shoes, socks, and trousers all over. And then they dried themselves in the sun.

The villagers never felt shy to ask me to help find city men as husbands for their daughters. That way, they said their daughters could have a chance to taste city life. "No matter if the men are lame or blind, so long as they get paid every month, we will let our daughters marry them," they always said.

Linlin had been gone for two months, but she didn't write. I missed her. Without Linlin life lost color. I felt alone and dull.

One afternoon Suansuan appeared at my door. I could hardly believe my eyes. She said she had met a horse cart which gave her a lift here.

I was very happy. "Suansuan, I have written you five letters. Did you receive all of them?"

"Yes, all. I'm very grateful. But I was not in a mood to write. I haven't touched my pen for many months. In my village, we worked all year round in the rice pond. They grow rice three times a year."

"I hate to work in the pond. The leeches are terrible."

"I hate everything in the countryside. I hate every peasant in the countryside. I hate everything on this land," Suansuan spat out the words.

We began to eat supper, fried eggs and green beans. Under the dim oil lamp Suansuan saw my English dictionary and my diary. She asked, "Do you still write?"

"Yes. But my writing is no good. I wish I had your talent. Your words are beautiful and your poetry expresses yourself so exquisitely."

"It's gone. All gone. I stopped writing. I hate everything. If I wrote, I would write everything against them."

"Suansuan, I met two writers. They both encouraged me to write." And I showed her my letters from Tao Kuang and Tian Yuan.

"Tian Yuan, the famous Sichuan poet? His real name is Zhang Pingyao. How did you meet him?"

"At the asbestos mines near Tibet."

"He is a gifted young man. He was in jail for some time."

"How do you know so much about him?"

"I've read his autobiography. I respect him very much."

After she finished reading his letter, she commented, "He loves you."

We were both silent. Then Suansuan asked, "Do you

still write to him?"

"No, I don't want to have a close relationship with a man." I thought of Deng He . . .

"I understand," she said. "Love is a miserable thing. But you missed a chance. He is worthy of love."

I didn't say anything. I didn't want to talk about love. In my heart, in the deepest place, there was still Deng He.

"I'm in love," Suansuan continued. "He's a rightist, but I love him." After a while she added, "In this world I love him only." Tears welled up in her eyes. "But they won't allow me to marry him. They said a rightist should not be in love."

I brought her tea. It was midnight.

"If one day I can earn twenty yuan a month, I will marry him," Suansuan declared.

"Suansuan, I hope you will get a factory job soon." I knew that a rightist could get no pay at all.

"I'll try. First, I will do my best to offend all the peasants, including all the peasant leaders."

"Why?"

"When I offend them they will chase me out of the countryside, and maybe in that way I'll become a factory worker."

Suansuan showed me her sunglasses and said, "I wore these glasses in my village, and played my mouth organ while walking around the fields. I wanted them to see me this way. I wanted to make them angry."

"Suansuan!" I became worried. "Please be careful. When all of them get angry they might hurt you. They may do something very cruel. Please be very careful."

By the time I woke up next morning, Suansuan had already left.

After a while all the factories stopped hiring students.

It's said that the factory leaders were angry because the commune leaders refused to send them the good city students. Instead, they sent only those who had paid bribes.

Summer came again, and we cut wheat in the fields again. This year it was extremely hot. To avoid the sun, we worked at night instead of in the daytime. Sometimes we started at one o'clock in early morning and continued to ten. Because of working in the dark, many villagers accidentally cut their hands.

One day I went to the brigade co-op to buy salt and I happened to see Gui Gui—the candidate for Vice Party Secretary of the brigade, the young man who had often bribed the Party secretary with baskets of eggs.

"How do you do?" he greeted.

"I'm fine."

"I heard you're a famous barefoot doctor and you can speak English. Could you teach me English?" he said and showed me a nice smile. He looked young, no more than twenty. I wondered how such a young boy could have developed into a briber. Wasn't it sad to see our new generation corrupted by such a society?

He paid me an unexpected visit the next day. He said, "I will help carry your firewood home from the mountain. And I will help you plant vegetables on your free land. But in return, you must teach me English."

"I don't have free land, but tell me, why do you want to study English?" I asked.

"For fun. It would be fun to speak English."

I taught him a few letters of the alphabet that day. Then I told him I would not teach anyone who studied English just for fun. "If you want to study, you must study hard and do the homework I give you and I'll check it." Gui Gui never asked me again.

After working at night for three weeks we had cut all the wheat and I was exhausted. They allowed us to take a few days off. I decided to visit my cousin Shong, the son of my father's sister. He was thirty-eight and lived with his wife in Zigong county twenty miles away. He was the Party Secretary of the Zigong Fertilizer Factory.

It was late afternoon when I arrived on the train, and I saw a noisy crowd of factory workers playing cards in the yard. "Hi, you must have washed your feet clean," Cousin Shong's wife greeted me from the kitchen. "You're walking into a banquet."

I went to the kitchen and saw Cousin Shong busily making dishes. "What kind of banquet are you preparing?" I asked.

"Twelve courses and a soup," he said.

"I've only heard of nine courses at most for a banquet. What's the occasion? Why twelve courses, and with a soup?"

Cousin Shong's wife said, "For entertainment. We hold a banquet every week. It's fun."

"For fun? How could you find the time."

"These days," she said, "We have nothing to do in the factory."

Cousin Shong was slicing fresh vegetables. I asked, "Cousin Shong, when did you learn how to cook?"

"During the Cultural Revolution."

"Thanks to the glorious Cultural Revolution. It can even produce chefs!" I joked.

"Don't say the Cultural Revolution is glorious," his wife said, "Your Cousin Shong has suffered a lot. He was in jail for a month, and sent down to a farm to feed pigs for half a year."

"Why was he put in jail? Did he support the rebel Red

Guards?" I asked.

"Right. He spoke up for the rebel Red Guards in his factory once or twice."

Cousin Shong said nothing. He just concentrated on the food preparation.

"In jail Cousin Shong ate water waves every day," his wife said.

"What's that?" I asked.

"It's called rice porridge, but it's just cloudy water."

"Cousin Shong, what do you think China's future will be like?"

He smiled, "I don't know."

"What are you doing in the factory now?" I asked again.

His wife said, "A monk striking the temple's bell."

"What do you mean?"

"We go to the factory every day to make an appearance," she explained. "Then we come home. Isn't that just like a monk striking the temple's bell once a day?"

"You mean workers don't work at all in the factory?"

"No. Because the government policies change so fast that nobody can catch up with them. The policy that was right yesterday becomes wrong today. The policy that is regarded as right today will be wrong tomorrow. We don't want to make mistakes about them. You know, because your Cousin Shong followed the policy of supporting the rebel Red Guards during the movement he was put in jail. People say, catching government policies is like catching public buses. The one in the morning is different from the one in the afternoon."

More than twenty guests were at the dinner table, all factory workers. They used revolutionary slogans to joke with each other while eating. "The working class is the leading class in China." "We would rather eat communist weeds than capitalist grain." A worker raised a wine cup and exclaimed, "We'd prefer drinking communist water to this capitalist wine."

After dinner, we all went to the theater for a free show, titled "Chairman Mao's Recreation Propaganda Performance."

The show was actually good, although most of the items were from the Eight Revolutionary Model Operas. When I discovered some of the actors and actresses were students, I asked myself, "Why not join them? To sing songs on the theater stage is better than working in the dull fields."

Cousin Shong's wife told me that all the actors lived just five blocks away from their house. The leader of the troupe was Chief Xi of the town's Bureau of Industry. I decided to see him next morning.

Chief Xi accepted me into his group after I auditioned for him with a folk song. He asked me to perform in the theater that very evening. At the theater, when I finished my song, the audience stood up and applauded until I finished three encores. Chief Xi looked very pleased. He urged me, "Hurry home to pack and return as soon as possible." He also promised he would pay me twenty-one yuan a month, and would allow me to go to a factory or study in a university if I got a chance.

The next day I took a train back to my village.

As I finished gathering my clothes together to depart, three people entered my house, the Party Secretary of the commune, the Party Secretary of the Brigade and Zhong Fong, the woman team leader.

The commune Party Secretary spoke first, "We have received a telephone call from Chief Xi, and we want to talk with you about your future. Would you like to be our commune school teacher? You can teach any class you like.

You can teach English."

Before I could say a word, he continued: "There is another choice for you. You can be a doctor in our commune hospital." Thoughts surged through my mind. All this happened so suddenly that I needed time to think and adjust. "We like you. All the villagers like you. We want you to stay with us." He finished, waiting for an answer from me.

The Brigade Party Secretary gave a signal to Zhong Fong, and she spoke, "You shouldn't be so arrogant. You must understand you came to the countryside to receive re-education. To tell you the truth, we don't want you to leave the countryside."

I didn't turn my eyes to her. I hated her manner. I didn't look at the Brigade Party Secretary either; I detested what he stood for—a corrupt official.

The commune Party Secretary spoke again, "Our commune values you. Please stay here. I will pay you twenty-one yuan a month. And, in one year, I will transfer your name from the village residence book to the city book. If there is any chance for university study I will recommend you first."

They all looked at me, waiting for an answer. I knew I didn't really have any other choice but to stay in the commune, so I said, "I'd like to teach English in the commune school."

They seemed relieved and the Party Secretary patted my shoulder, saying, "You can teach anything you like."

"Will you really transfer my name from the village residence book to the city book?" I asked him.

"Certainly. I promise."

"Why will it take such a long time for you to do it?"

The brigade leader spoke for him, "Because you have

not been in the countryside long enough."

I followed the Party Secretary to the commune school.

The school was a cluster of old gray-brick structures located between two small mountains, with a narrow river in the front. When I arrived, all the teachers came out and stood at the school gate.

"A new teacher for you," the commune Party Secretary announced and gave me a big smile.

Among the teachers I spotted Mr. Huang, the political commissar with whom I had worked in the bandit village years before. He grasped my hands, "Welcome, welcome, little comrade, I am so happy to see you again." He was a principal here, he told me. He introduced me to the other teachers, "This little comrade is a great person. You'll see!" The teachers stared at me. They seemed cold.

Principal Huang showed me to my apartment, actually a little single room, and told me he had just been transferred to this school a month ago. The living quarters consisted of some old rooms joined together, with no floors. All the teachers lived in there, door-to-door, sharing a cement yard in the center. My room was very bright inside because the window was twice as large as the door, with no curtain. No teacher had a private kitchen. Principal Huang told me that all the teachers ate together in the school dining room at a specific time.

To the right of the rooms was the school playground. Beyond, was the wooden office building, tall, gray and in shambles. It looked somewhat like an old temple. Work hours were from 8 a.m. to 9 p.m. During that time the teachers were not allowed to go to their rooms.

There were two red, two story classroom buildings behind the office. Principal Huang asked me to teach English, Chinese literature, and Chinese history. The next day I received my textbooks.

The first lesson in English was a single sentence: "Long Live Chairman Mao." The second was: "We wish Chairman Mao a long, long life." The third was: "Chairman Mao is our great leader." The Chinese literature textbook began: "Shaoshan, Chairman Mao's place of birth." On the first page of the Chinese history book I read: "The history of human beings is the history of class struggles. One class wipes out another to push history forward." All were quotations from Mao.

I started to regret the decision to teach here. But, when I stood before the class, seeing sixty earnest faces looking up at me, I felt my responsibility to them and I told myself, "I am a teacher. My duty is to share my knowledge with these students." For the first class in English, instead of teaching a political slogan, I taught them the alphabet. I created a song to help them remember it.

I loved Chinese literature, so in my Chinese class I often read to the students some of the great Tang poems, and stories from *The Dream of the Red Chamber,* and other Chinese classics. I was cautious, though, and each time before I read to them I said, "This is just for criticism." I required them to write diaries, too, which I checked and corrected every day.

The students seemed to enjoy the history class very much. They were excited and proud to learn that our ancestors invented gunpowder, printing and the compass. They also liked to ask me why all the emperors in history were so cruel and stupid. My answer was, "Think. Use your own head. You'll find out some day."

To enrich my students' lives, I taught them ballet, which I had learned from Linlin. I danced badly, but better than they could. In the afternoon, after formal classes, I usually taught them how to train their voices for singing. They seemed to especially enjoy this.

Principal Huang approved my ways of teaching. At faculty meetings he frequently remarked that I was a good teacher and that he was proud of me. His wife was kind to me too, and treated me as one of her own children.

Among the teachers I felt very close to was Teacher Chang, a chemistry instructor of about forty. She was the only university graduate in the school, and she enjoyed music, as I did. Many evenings when I played the Chinese piano (pump organ) she came to join me and sang along. Her husband, a very brilliant man, graduated from a famous university, but had been forced to teach in a small village school far away in the mountains because he had been dubbed a rightist in 1957.

I also liked Teacher Shi, an elderly man who taught agriculture. He had once been the principal of the school, but he was labelled a rightist in 1957, and lost the principal's chair. He played piano beautifully and he painted well. His wife, a pretty lady, taught in a brigade school nearby.

I despised the math teacher. She was rude to the students. If a student didn't speak loudly enough for her in class she would curse right away, saying something like "What pig hair is stuck in your throat?" If a student asked for drinking water, she would say, "Water? Water or urine?" Besides this, she was incompetent. She taught many formulas incorrectly, which I discovered by checking my students' homework. Believing it a duty to my students, I held math classes for them every Saturday afternoon. I also reported the problem to Principal Huang, saying, "She is not a qualified teacher."

Principal Huang opened his two hands in a gesture of defeat and said, "I can do nothing. I know she is not qualified. She didn't even finish high school."

"Then why is she allowed to teach high school students?"

"The commune decided. I had no choice."

"We must be responsible to the students. They are the children of the peasants. They are the commune's future!"

"I'm afraid I can do nothing," he replied.

Later, I learned that the math teacher was a member of the Communist Party and that she had relatives in the commune leadership. I couldn't respect her and found it hard to conceal my feeling.

I often went to the villages to visit the homes of my students and to meet their parents. When students were sick I went to see them no matter whether it was raining or stifling hot. Some students lived so far away I had to walk over four hills, which took several hours each way. The families were all quite poor. But they were always kind to me, and wanted to cook special dishes in honor of the visit. I didn't want them to go to such trouble, so I started carrying bread with me when I made those visits.

Half a year passed, and I became close to all my students and their families. But the irregularity of meals and constant cold food started giving me stomach trouble. Often I would double over in the class from the pain.

A year passed. I enjoyed being a teacher, and liked to imagine that some day when all my students would grow up and become experts in English, Chinese history, or Chinese literature, I would be proud to say I had been their teacher.

One day I read in the government newspapers that all the universities were going to reopen. I could hardly believe my eyes, I was so excited. How I wished I could go immediately. Then I heard that the Shanghai Foreign Languages Institute was going to choose a student from our commune. I was certain I would be the candidate.

A week later I met Gui Gui by chance. He announced he was going to Shanghai.

"Visiting?" I asked.

"No, I was recommended by the commune to study foreign languages at the Institute for three years. Now all the universities are open for Worker-Peasant-Soldier students. As a Worker-Peasant-Soldier student you don't have to have graduated from high school. You know, the commune recommended me because my hands have thick callouses."

My chance for studying was lost. A heavy sadness pressed against me. I felt cheated and betrayed.

A few days later, Principal Huang summoned me to his office. He looked pale and told me the commune had ordered me back to my previous village to become a peasant again.

"What?" I asked. I couldn't believe it. "The three leaders promised to transfer my name to the city residence book. That time has come."

"Things have changed."

"What do you mean?"

"I don't know how to explain it to you. It's best you ask the commune Party Secretary.

I rushed to the commune office, and knocked on the door. "What made all of you deceive me into teaching here?" I demanded of the commune Party Secretary.

"Nobody cheated you."

"Then why are you breaking your promise?"

"There was no promise. Everything is changing. And you have changed, too."

"Explain that!" I demanded.

"You have not united with the advanced teachers in your school. You are arrogant to them, especially to the math teacher. You got involved with rightist teachers. You made friends only with them. Where is your political awareness? Which way do you want to go? Socialism or Capitalism?"

I was shaking and nearly fainted. I didn't know what I would say.

"The most serious mistake you have made is to allow a rightist man to carry you on his back," he finished.

I turned and rushed out. How could I explain? Teacher Shi had once carried me on his back to the hospital because, on that day, I had suddenly fallen ill while in class. My students had asked him to help take me to the hospital because he happened to teach in the next classroom.

This is the end. Everything is over. Sitting alone in my room, I thought of death.

Evening came, I opened the door and walked towards the river.

CHAPTER 19

Recovery

復 - 蘇

When I woke, I found myself lying on a bed in the commune hospital. I was told the commune had changed its mind, and had transferred my name from the village residence book to that of the city. Teacher Chang said I had been rescued from the river by a peasant and that I had already been in the hospital for three days. She told me many students and their parents had come to see me and had reported this matter to the district and city governments. As a result they had sent groups to the commune to investigate the matter and sharply criticized the commune leaders.

Principal Huang visited me in the hospital and gave me much kind advice. "You must add another string to your head," he said. "Every human brain is like an instrument formed by complex strings and your instrument is too simple. You are too naive."

He went on, "Don't you know that our society is complicated and filled with class struggles? Don't you remember Chairman Mao's teaching: 'Never forget class struggle,' and 'Always place politics in command'? You must be aware that the relationship between man and man in our society is political rather than personal."

The commune Party Secretary came to see me, too. He brought me fruit and candy, and he apologized. He also explained that he didn't mean to hurt me that day. "I didn't know you felt so hurt. You mustn't do that kind of thing again. You are young, your life is just beginning. You must make yourself strong and make your stomach able to hold much, to hold all the different opinions of different people. Remember the saying, 'A brave man's stomach can hold ships.'"

Then he told me a story about himself. "At the beginning of the Cultural Revolution they accused me of having sexual relationships with nine women and demanded I confess at the Party member meetings. I didn't, of course. Then they dragged me to a struggle meeting with hundreds of peasants present. In the meeting I fought back. I am an old Communist Party member. I know I must speak the facts. I can't lie. One of the principles for a communist is not to lie. You know, because I spoke the facts, I won."

He took my hand and said, "You must speak out what is in your stomach. Speak out, and you'll feel better. And when you speak out, people can hear and can help you. People are not fish. Everyone has a brain. Everyone can think and decide for himself what is right and what is wrong."

He took my hands in his as he said goodbye. "Look at your arms, they are so thin. How can such thin arms carry burdens? I should say your arms haven't enough strength to carry a chicken." We both smiled. "One more thing," he said, "according to our Communist Party, it is a criminal act to commit suicide."

I gradually recovered, and realized I had been foolish to try to kill myself. Grass can grow up from under a rock, why not me? God creating me, must have wanted me to do something on this earth.

Principal Huang held a tea party to welcome me back to school and I was told the school had decided to let me give lectures on Chinese literature once a week for all the teachers as additional work. I taught the same classes as before. The math teacher seemed changed, and she invited me to her wedding. I wanted to tell her, "I want to be your friend. I will give you my high school math books, and I will help you go through all of them." But, somehow, in the end, I could never make myself say a word.

My students had been very close to me, and were now even closer. They said I had never hurt them, which pleased me.

My students wrote me lovely letters. Before he moved to another city, a boy paid me a special visit. He gave me a gift, his diary, in which he wrote: "My dear teacher, you are my most beloved teacher. You spread learning wheat to your students, and carefully tend them—watering, fertilizing, pulling weeds away and loosening the soil. When we all grow up we will become great shafts of wheat to serve all the hungry people in the world."

Cousin Song's family lived not far from my school, and they often invited me to spend holidays with them. There I gradually grew more and more interested in learning to cook well because both my cousin and his wife were very good at cooking. They liked to hold banquets on weekends. Cooking had been fun for them since the Cultural Revolution broke out. And I became a good cook under their instruction.

I called my cousin's wife Cousin Sister. She was a very warm person and very kind to me. She kept asking me one question: "Have you found a boyfriend?"

"Yes," I always answered. This was the one thing I never wanted to talk about.

"What is he doing? Is he handsome? How did you meet him?"

"I won't tell you until the time is right."

One day she insisted I tell her about my boyfriend and I said, "He is short, quite fat and a heavy smoker."

She exclaimed, "My goodness, why do you choose a man like that? How can your parents tolerate a heavy smoker?"

Before I could say anything, she asked, "Really decided? That's terrible!"

I didn't have a boy friend, of course. I had been describing Mr. Xiong, the Beijing Red Guard. He had never said that he loved me.

"Where is he now?" Cousin Sister continued to question. "In Heilongjiang," I answered. "I heard that he had been sent to Heilongjiang, the coldest part of China, to be a farmer as punishment by his university because he was a rebel Red Guard leader during the Cultural Revolution."

She seemed to want to ask something more about him, but I hinted that I didn't want to talk any more on that subject.

Winter was coming. Cousin Sister sewed me a padded jacket, purple in color, and made me a white sweater. In the evening stroll she said to me, "Remember, purple is your color. I will make you a purple sweater, and next summer I will sew you a purple skirt. You never care about your dress. That is wrong. You know, if you had cared about your dress, you would have found a handsome man instead of that heavy smoker."

I laughed. Her advice sounded interesting but funny.

The next weekend when I visited my cousin's family, both my cousin and his wife started talking about a medical researcher named Mr. Chen. "He is our friend," my cousin said. "An honest man, twenty-nine years old. He graduated from Nanking Medical University in 1965. Because he was the top student, he was assigned by the government to the Beijing Institute of Basic Medical Sciences, the best medical institute in China. At the beginning of the Cultural Revolution, when Chairman Mao set up the Six-Twenty-Six Medical Policy, Mr. Chen, with hundreds of his colleagues, moved into our town."

I remembered that policy. It ordered all the medical researchers, doctors, and nurses to leave the big cities and big hospitals for small cities and small hospitals.

Cousin Sister said, "Two Sichuan colleagues brought him to visit us since he has no relatives in Sichuan. He is a single man from Wuxi in Jiangsu Province. He is very kind. When he heard that your aunt was sick, he went to her hospital to see her. We like him very much, and we will try to help him find a good girl so he can settle down here.

Then my cousin asked me seriously, "Do you know any good person in your school?" My cousin had never tried to do anything like this before. He must have really cared very much about this medical man, I thought.

She added, "You must find a pretty young girl, a professional person as a match for Dr. Chen. He is very good-looking."

It happened that I did know a pretty and gentle music teacher at my neighborhood school. Her name was Xiao Liao. She was twenty-two and came from a county official's family. Her parents were both gracious and educated. Xiao Liao said she was interested in meeting Dr. Chen and urged me to take her to my cousin's home the following week.

Dr. Chen and his two professors were sitting in the living room. He was neatly dressed, clearly a gentleman, and he wore glasses. After we all were introduced, I went to another room to read the newspapers. But before I had finished the first page, Xiao Liao came in, looking sad, and told me Dr. Chen was not interested in her, and she said goodbye.

That evening, when Cousin Sister joined me in my daily stroll, she told me Dr. Chen and his two professors had asked much about me after Xiao Liao left.

"They must be interested in my purple jacket," I joked. "I should have had Xiao Liao wear my jacket this morning." We both laughed.

Half a year passed. It was 1973. I had almost completely forgotten about Dr. Chen, when my cousin wrote and urged me to visit them as soon as possible.

In the living room, both cousin and Cousin Sister looked serious. My cousin asked, "Do you really have a boy friend or not? Tell us the truth."

"No," I answered. "Why?"

They both seemed relieved, and, as I drank tea, my cousin asked, "Do you remember Dr. Chen? He likes you."

I was surprised and a little bit embarrassed. So I made a joke to relax. "He liked my purple jacket, didn't he?"

My cousin looked into my eyes and asked, "Would you like to consider him your lifetime friend?"

I was startled. How could I find a lifetime friend this way? I looked at him earnestly and answered, "I don't think so."

My cousin continued, "He is a good man, a responsible person. I think you should take him into your consideration." He looked at me with compassion. For the first time I realized that he looked like my father. Then he said, "I have checked his background. My wife and I visited his institute three times. People there called him Iron Man, because he has been very brave during these years of the Cultural Revolution. You know how the intellectuals have been tormented throughout the revolution. He and more than eighty new medical graduates were accused of being Capitalist Stinking Number Nines. The professors in the institute suffered the most. A woman professor was beaten to death in a struggle meeting. Many professors committed suicide, and one professor swallowed needles to kill himself. Under such pressures, many students made false accusations and confessions, but Dr. Chen did not. Even at struggle meetings in which there were hundreds of people, he would fight back. Then they tried to deal with him by putting him under house arrest. For six months he was guarded day and night. They didn't allow him to send or receive letters to or from his friends or family, even his aged parents. But he still refused to 'confess' to anything. To punish him they made him clean toilets in the institute."

As I listened to him, I admired Dr. Chen more and more. I respect bravery in a person. I knew the Cultural Revolution, and I knew to be brave in that time was no easy matter. A young man of twenty-three so brave was rare.

Cousin continued, "Since the Cultural Revolution has not yet ended, the military group in leadership at his institute recently ordered all intellectuals to become barefoot doctors for one year in the Ningxia Hui Autonomous Region. Dr. Chen went there with two hundred of his colleagues. Before he left town, he paid us a visit. He told us that he liked you very much."

I tried to recall what he looked like. I remembered his deep melodic voice, and that he sat up very straight the day he came to visit. His neck seemed a bit longer than most people's. I seemed to remember his eyes, although he had glasses on. His eyes were not big, but clear, and in them a slight sadness.

Cousin Sister put in, "He plays many musical instruments. He draws well, and at the institute his calligraphy was rated the best. He is a philosopher too. People in his institute said he had read a great deal of philosophy and history."

She added, "Let me tell you, this man is perfect. You will not find a better man, even if you search day and night."

Has fate sent this man to me? I asked myself. Why am I attracted to him, to his qualities and talents? It was true. I had never known anyone who could compare with him in any respect. This is the man I should love, I said to myself. At least, I wanted us to become friends. So I agreed to my cousin writing to him.

A month later I received a letter from Dr. Chen. His handwriting was unusually graceful. He told me so many things about himself, his family and his hometown, Wuxi, one of the most beautiful places in China. He had deep feelings for his parents and hometown. He told me that, as a barefoot doctor, he had to walk over five hills every day to see his patients. They were all shepherds or the tenders of horses. The area had vegetable shortages and water shortages, so nearly every meal was mutton stew, and he washed his face with the same water for several days. But, he told me, he loved the people there, poor yet simple and sincere. In the evenings he sometimes slept in the horse-tender's tent.

I wrote back immediately, telling him about my school, my parents, and my friends.

The letter took a month to get to him, so I decided to

send him a telegram once a week.

He wrote to me once a week, and sometimes he wrote me a song. "I play it on my *San Xuan* at night when I am alone. I miss you." One day he drew me a picture of a cow with a little child sitting on its back playing a flute. Over the picture he wrote, "On the way home." It was a peaceful picture that deeply moved me. "Home," I thought, how many people really know the meaning of "home"? Home for me, and for him, is everything, also beyond everything; a dream beyond a dream. It is a place where we can be completely ourselves.

In another letter he told me, "When I was a child I was always afraid of darkness. At night I wanted my mother with me. The most comfortable moment in my memory is sleeping in my mother's arms where I had no worry, and where I felt safe. For many years the word 'mother' meant to me the same as the word 'home.'"

Sometimes he called me "Sunshine" when he wrote to me. "Your name can be explained also as Morning Sunshine," he wrote. "Your character is like your name. You have warmed my heart."

We continued to write like this, telling almost everything about our lives. We wrote poems to each other, made up fairy tales about our hometowns. We talked about history, art, literature, philosophy . . . but we never said a word about the Cultural Revolution. It was too painful to look back, we knew. The future is ours, and the future is hopeful.

One year later we married and set up our own home.
. . . A new life began. We love each other, respect each other and encourage each other's careers.

We have a beautiful daughter, Yang Yang (Sunshine). She is loving and sensitive, and often says, "My mother is the moon and I am the moonlight."

Epilogue

拔

In 1975 I was transferred to a city school near my husband's institute. It was a big school with sixty-five teachers. I taught Chinese literature, history, chemistry, music and English, twenty-four hours a week. All the teachers there were lively and friendly. They even talked freely about political matters.

Our beloved Premier Zhou died in January 1976. When the news came over the local radio station the teachers wept. In the past, whenever a high official passed away, our work units would buy black arm bands of mourning and distribute them among the working personnel. The work unit would also hold an official, solemn commemoration meeting. Yet when Premier Zhou died, no leader mentioned any of this. Well, we didn't care what the leadership wanted or didn't want. We bought our own black cloth and made arm bands for ourselves and family members. We set up an office as a memorial hall and placed hand-made wreathes of white paper flowers and evergreen branches there. Our school principal tried to read out a tribute, but her voice was choked with tears. When students arrived, each also wore a white flower and a black arm band they had made themselves.

On September 9, 1976, Chairman Mao Zedong died. He was 83 years old. The local government assigned all the units, offices, factories, schools, etc., to set up memorial halls, and each hall was to be guarded at night to express deep loyalty to Mao. I was pregnant then and my on-duty hours were from 12 midnight to 2 a.m. Some other teachers had even worse hours: 2 to 4 a.m. or 4 to 6 a.m. We were told it was forbidden to smile, chat, or play cards when we were on duty. Disobedience to these rules meant arrest for not being serious. My husband, worried about my health, took over my guard duty.

Rumor had it that Chairman Mao left a will stating: "I've done two things in my life—one was to drive out the Guomindang and the other was to launch the Cultural Revolution. Few people supported this Cultural Revolution; many opposed it. The Cultural Revolution is not yet finished, but in this bloody turmoil I have no more time left and can only leave it for someone else to carry on."

On October 6, 1976, less than a month after Mao's death, a big school meeting was held. At this, our principal announced: "A revolutionary action has been taken by our government!" He went on to read the official proclamation, which stated that Jiang Qing (Mao's wife), Huang Hongwen, Zhang Chunqiao, and Yao Wenyuan ("the gang of four") were all arrested by the 8341 Guard Unit, whose duty was to safeguard the Zhongnanhai residences and the offices of the officials of the Communist Party Central Government.

As soon as this meeting was over, everyone dashed out to spread the joyous news, and to buy wine and peanuts. That evening we held a big banquet in the school playground to celebrate. Many students joined us.

Comrade Deng Xiaoping came to power in 1977 and, among other things, restored the system of taking a national examination for college entrance. I took the examination and was accepted by Sichuan Teacher's University. I left my daughter with my parents and went to study English for four years. During that time, I was able to visit my daughter and my husband, each, only once a year.

I graduated in 1981 and got a job as a teacher and translator in Beijing Union Medical University, where my husband had become an assistant professor of pathology.

In August 1985, I came to the United States as a visiting scholar to conduct further studies in English literature.

My friend Suansuan had a mental breakdown, and remains in the hospital. She had worked in a mountain village for eight years. She never married. Fang Mei's fate was much happier. After the Cultural Revolution Fang and his wife, the girl I had mailed the letter to who was a high school graduate and violin player, came to visit me. Both said "It was your kind help that made our present happiness possible." Fang explained that his brother was a high-level official in the central government in Beijing. When his brother received the letter I'd mailed, he sent people to Sichuan to get Fang released immediately.

As soon as it was possible, I tried to find Tao Kuang, my dear friend from Mount Emei. I sent out many letters to wherever I thought she might be. But I never heard from her again. I will never forget her. She was the first person to encourage me to write. It was she who told me: "Write honestly, because life itself is honest."